FATMA BUCAK

# While the Dust Quickly Falls

Kunsthaus Dresden Mousse Publishing

WORKS

***Numbing silence covers us like fine dust*** / 1–4, 13–16

***A tree*** / 33–39

***Damascus rose*** / 43–48

***Black Ink*** / 63, 65–67

***They burned it all*** / 77–85

***Hate to disturb this precious silence*** / 86, 91–93

***The gift of sight*** / 94–97

***An interlude*** / 26–27, 99–111

***Sum of the misdeeds and consents and cowardly acts*** / 112—119

***Perpetual lure and insistent fear*** / 120–126

TEXTS

**Foreword** / 9

Christiane Mennicke-Schwarz

**Ecological Grief** / 17

Kari Conte

**Dustwork** / 49

Eray Çaylı

**On Falling Quickly** / 69

Heather Davis

**Capitalocene in Prestissimo** / 87

Ecem Arslanay

Acknowledgements / 127

Colophon / 128

# Foreword

CHRISTIANE MENNICKE-SCHWARZ

Cinematographic abundance paired with a minimalist attention to material in its political dimension and human action are seemingly divergent strategies of Fatma Bucak's work. With these strategies, she addresses the loss of geopolitical and geo-cultural landscapes and forms a new vocabulary to describe the distinct human experience of fear, terror, love, and anxiety.

It was one of those rare moments in which shared interests and energies immediately clicked. When I first met Fatma in 2020, in Dresden in the middle of the pandemic, it quickly became apparent that the articulation of mourning and trauma as a fundamental human experience was a shared concern of ours. Fatma's works, through their precise use of imagery and material, function as allegories for the fragility of our existence. My first encounter with the aesthetics of these works was a touching and outstanding experience. A series of meaningful encounters and conversations followed while we were trying to overcome the great divide of the pandemic lockdown during her residency at the Foundation of Art and Music for Dresden. Kari Conte, who was introduced to me by Fatma, became the curator of the shared project and exceptional exhibition at Kunsthaus Dresden documented in this catalog, and soon joined these exchanges. Through her amazing knowledge, congenial inspiration, and empathic abilities, Kari became an important partner. Based on these conversations, which had started in the garden branch of Kunsthaus Dresden and later continued on digital platforms, Fatma expressed her vital interest in dedicating artistic research to the cultural and political heritage of healing in the Mediterranean and beyond, and to the ancient knowledge of planetary coexistence embedded in this heritage.

Fatma's travel and research, and the ensuing production of work, connected a remarkable group of individuals, collectives, and regions, thanks to the generous support of the Italian Council. Her exhibition, *While the Dust Quickly Falls* at Kunsthaus Dresden, is the result of extensive artistic research and a distinct aesthetic empathy for the conditions that shape the survival of non-human and human life—as well as hundreds of individual exchanges and encounters.

In *While the Dust Quickly Falls*, Fatma directs attention to regions and landscapes that are exemplary for shared geopolitical zones with a highly endangered ecological status. Zones that have suffered for decades from political conflict and humanmade climate change. Regions which in many respects are held to be the cradle of civilization and progress, and where now (in some cases for more than a century), political violence, exploitation, and neglect are eradicating ecological habitats as well as the basic conditions of human social cohesion.

The exhibition traces the evidence and ambivalence of human use of non-human resources, based on the example of the capacities of plants. The plants in the exhibition are medicinal, but at the same time they can be—and have been since ancient times—used for poison. The ash that results from a forest fire can—depending on the intensity of the fire—have a fertilizing effect. At the same time, fire can destroy the biodiversity and life in a region forever, leaving a wasteland and decimating the non-human life of plants and animals and any base for human coexistence.

When we look at plants or soil in Fatma's exhibition, we are also looking directly at human communities and regions where a return to their original biodiversity seems impossible. Hundreds of thousands of hectares of forest have been destroyed in the last two years in Turkey and Greece. These fires are caused by the extreme rise in temperatures resulting from humanmade climate change, mismanagement, systematic neglect of Kurdish areas, and land speculation. And yet, the material aesthetics of Fatma's works and their extraordinarily poetic titles share a mode of individual lament rather than an immediate activist response.

Her work is about more than putting a finger in the wound, more even than the infinitely important work of mourning, which perhaps still lies ahead of us. Because all her works—and here lies the hopeful core—in the exhibition are about resistance and transformation, in the best sense of the word. The ashes of the books of a burned-down Kurdish publishing house become ink again in *Black Ink*. With the appropriate will, a new tree can grow from the remains of the destroyed forest. And from the torn language and the lament for the forest and all that is lost with it, a new song emerges. Especially in these times—when (yet another) war is devastating both people and landscapes in Ukraine and currently shaking our world—Fatma's work offers an important perspective, one that is essential for survival, of overcoming and transforming narratives of political violence.

Fatma's first encounter with Dresden was at the invitation of the Foundation of Art and Music for Dresden, and I am infinitely grateful to Martina de Maizière for introducing us and to the foundation for contributing to the development of the new works. I am extremely thankful that the Italian Council—an initiative of the Italian Ministry of Culture—through its generous support, also facilitated the beautiful and special collaboration that developed between Kari, Fatma, and our team, with Kerstin Flasche and myself as co-curatorial sparring partners. The jury of the Italian Council evaluated the artistic proposal as so meaningful that Fatma could work, travel, and conduct research for more than a year, with a total of seven new works created for the exhibition. Many of these works will go directly from the exhibition into the collection of MAMbo – Museo d'Arte Moderna di Bologna. I am particularly moved by the fact that the SAHA Association in Istanbul has also decided to support this artistic collaboration, focusing on the creation of this publication.

Much gratitude is owed to the authors of this catalog—Ecem Arslanay, Eray Çaylı, Kari Conte, and Heather Davis—for their thoughtful contributions, which dwell on the exhibition in light of climate change, dust, and conflict. With their essays, they bring some of the important strands of research in *While the Dust Quickly Falls* to life, addressing both its essential and exemplary cultural and political implications for our current global conditions. This catalog is designed by Esen Karol, who added a brilliant visual layer to the exhibition's material.

I would especially like to thank our team, at the forefront Peter Segor, for his technical support, and Kerstin Flasche. Freshly arrived as a vital new member of our institution and curatorial team for the project, Kerstin has managed this project in its many stages with scientific curiosity, organizational courage, and great personal responsibility. Hosting the temporary archive *An interlude*—with more than a hundred plants and keeping them alive for a three-month exhibition—brought the profession of "curator" to life in more than one respect. Our greatest thanks, of course, goes to Fatma and Kari for the amazing amount of trust, inspiration, and diligence that they invested in the process of research and curation, the unique aesthetic experience of the exhibition at Kunsthaus Dresden, and moreover, the editing of the publication we now hold in our hands.

*Christiane Mennicke-Schwarz is a curator and art historian and Director of Kunsthaus Dresden.*

p. 1–4, 13–16:

***Numbing silence covers us like fine dust***, 2022
Soil and ash collected from the 2021 Tunceli forest fires, wood, and sound
330 × 1,400 × 880 cm
Sound composition Bahar Royaee
Project realized with the support of the Italian Council (2022)

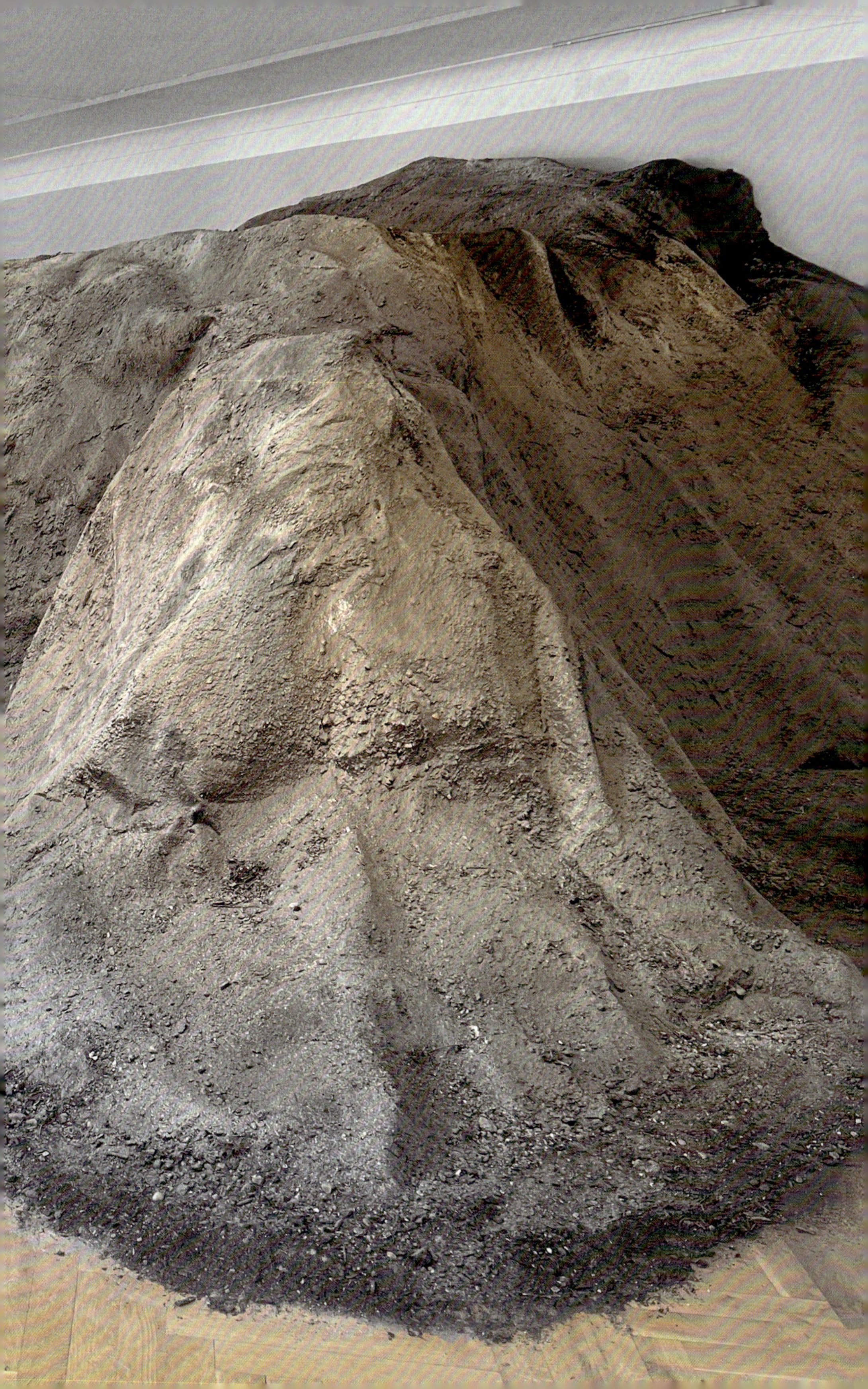

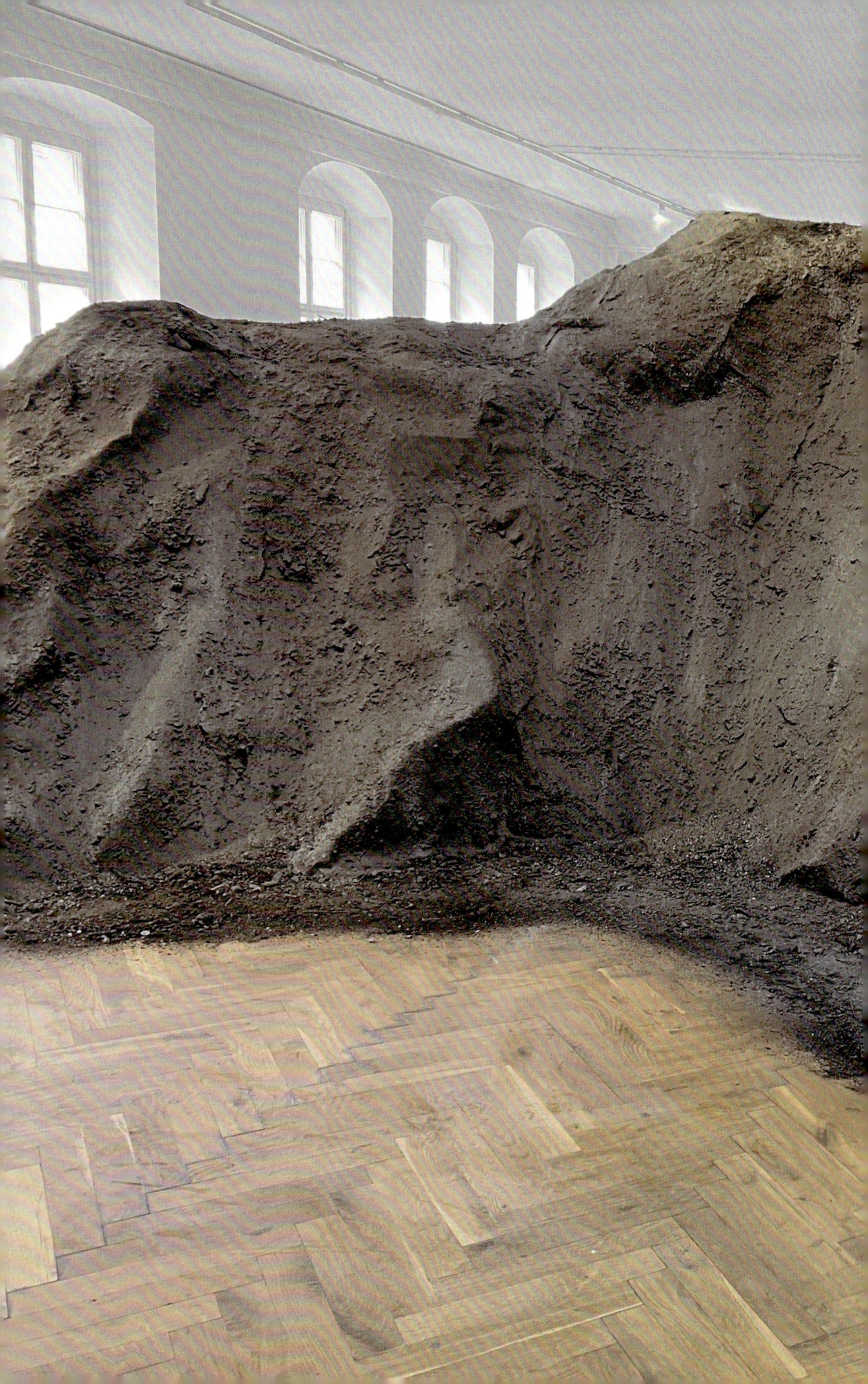

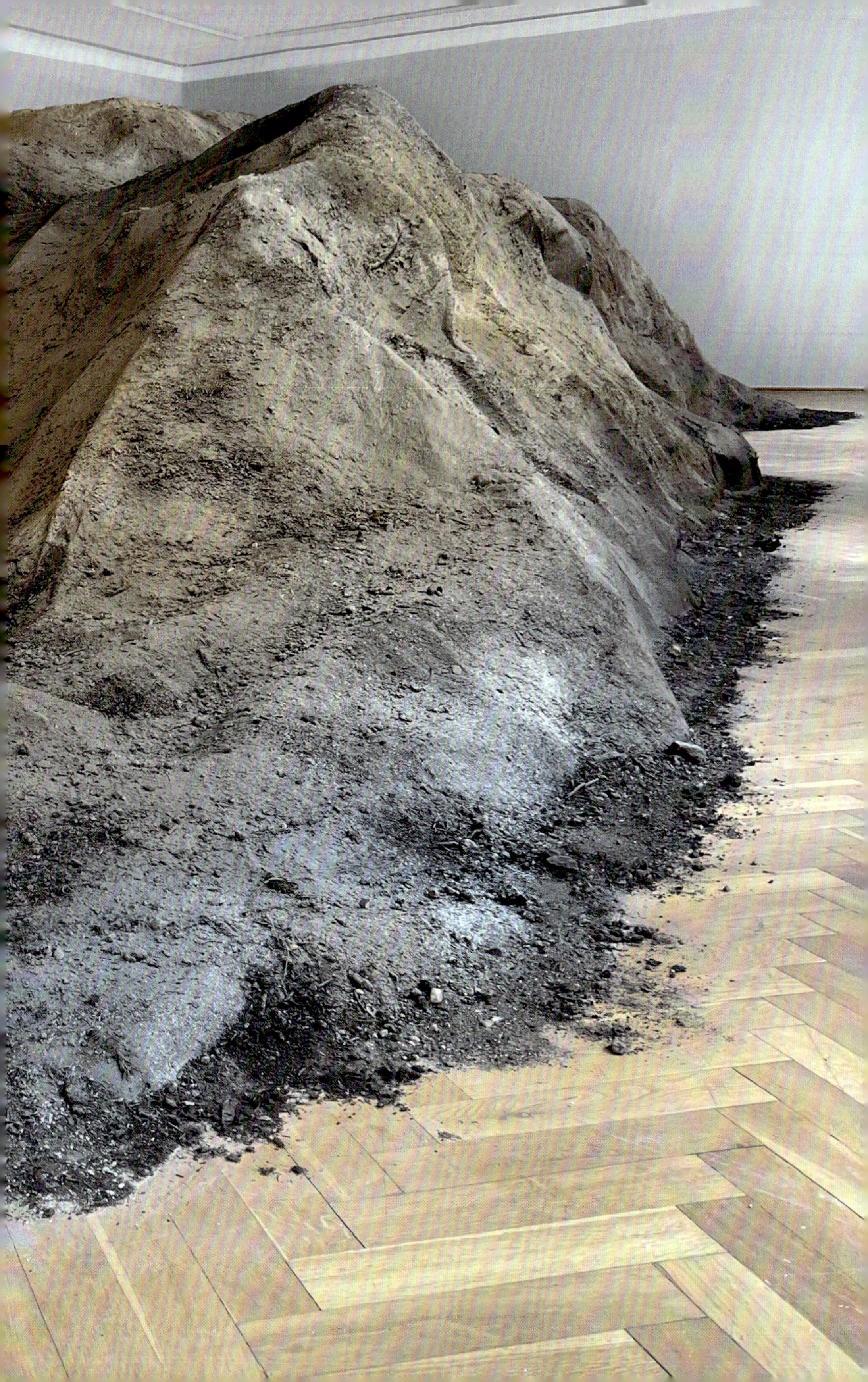

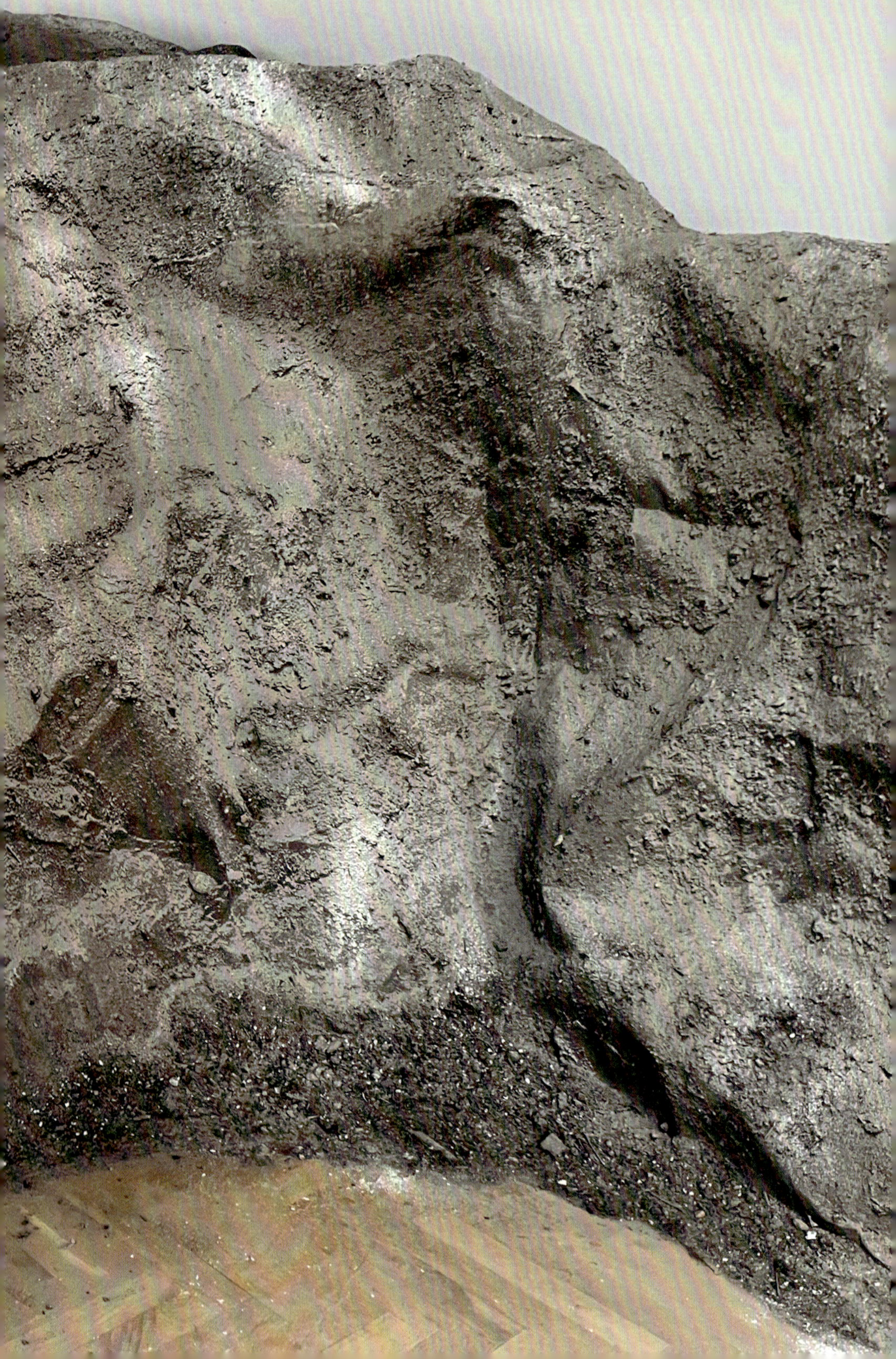

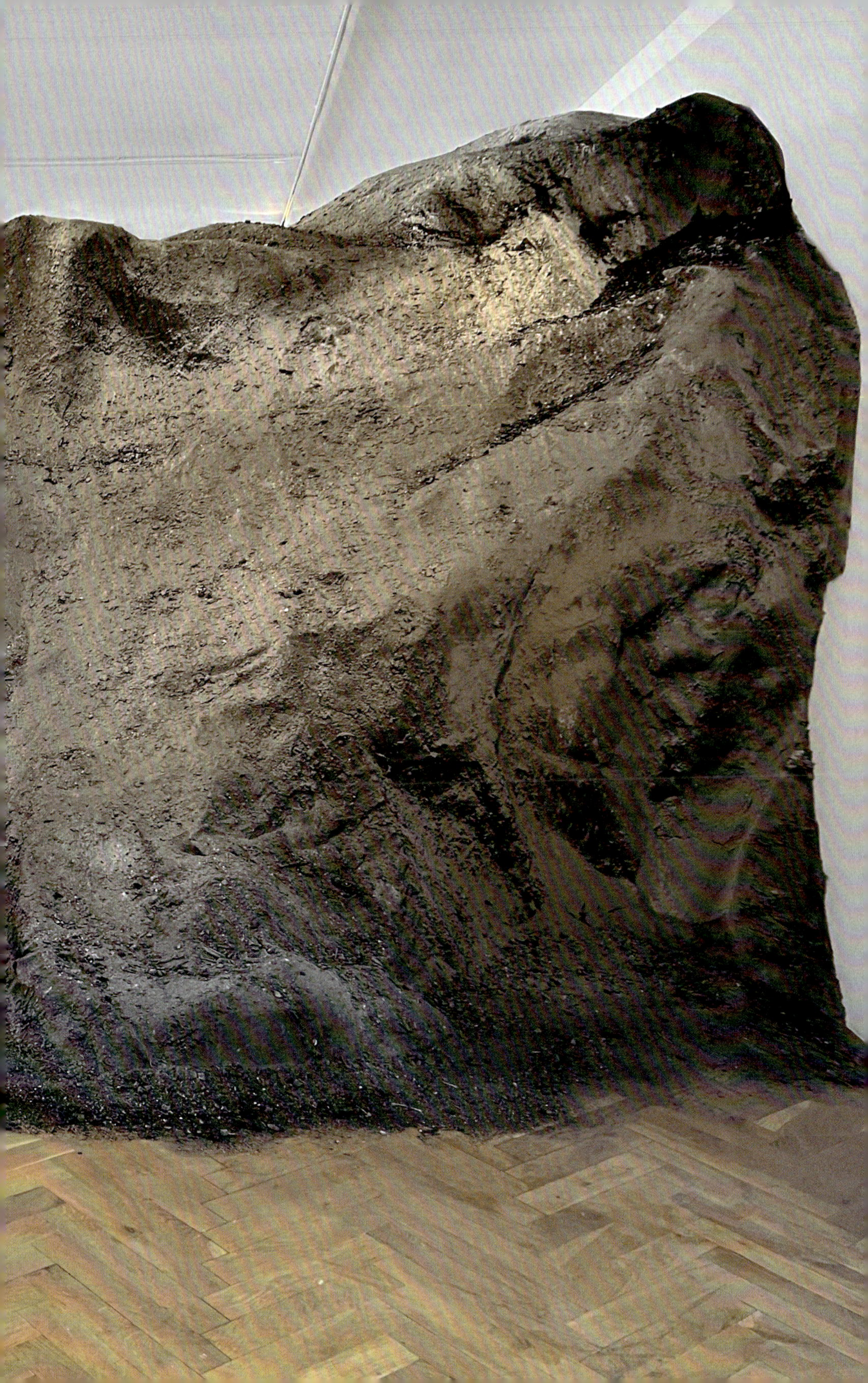

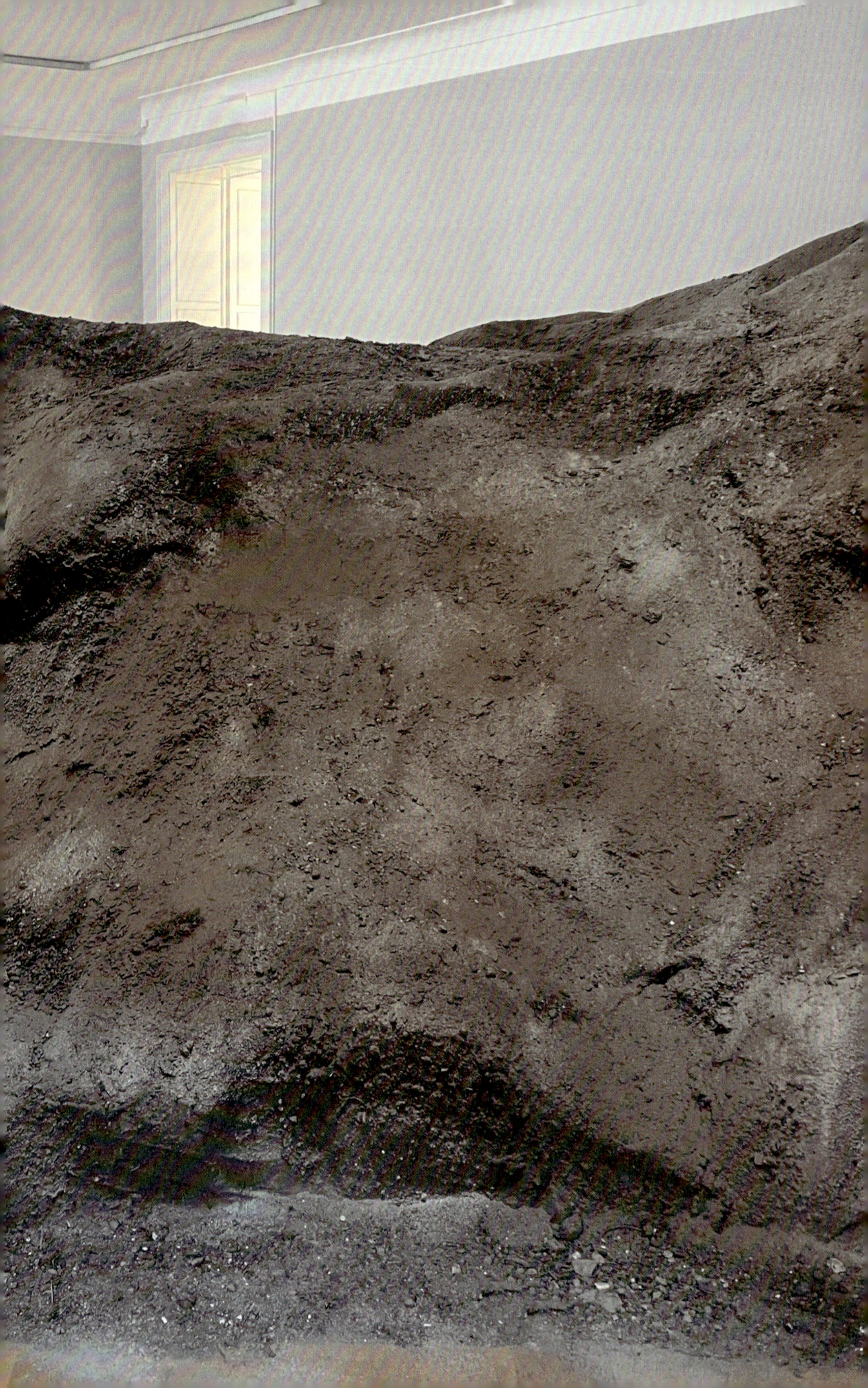

# Ecological Grief

KARI CONTE

In *While the Dust Quickly Falls*, artist Fatma Bucak invites us to consider how political violence accelerates environmental destruction and climate change, particularly in the Mediterranean region. Composed of new commissions and existing works reinterpreted for the Kunsthaus Dresden, the exhibition moves across disparate geographies—Eastern Anatolia, the Golan Heights, Damascus, Sardinia, Baghdad, and Istanbul—that are connected by the catastrophic impact that conflict and war have had on their ecologies. It dwells poetically on the loss of biodiversity, endangered and extinct plants, humanity's interdependence on non-human beings, and healing.

The ten works in the exhibition question how humanity is ethically implicated and entangled in ecological transformation and destruction. In her fieldwork for the exhibition, the artist traveled to regions in Turkey and Italy impacted by the sweeping 2021 Mediterranean forest fires, precipitated by extreme heatwaves and ongoing droughts. A burned forest is an abyss emptied of flourishing life, where the remaining life grasps for survival. During forest fires, uneven patches of land burn, and one side of a mountain, road, or river can be decimated while the other stands untouched. Moving through a scorched forest is an experience of both exhilaration and despair. After the 2021 forest fires in Turkey, I walked into several of the burned areas near my adopted home in the Bodrum Peninsula. I felt joy and relief for the swaths not leveled to debris and ashes. Yet, as I turned a corner or climbed higher, the landscape changed unexpectedly; the trees, other plants, and rocks were ravaged and split apart. I experienced ecological grief arising from permanent loss, which is, in a way, the feeling of being homesick, even when you are still home. Before me, the ruins of once-thriving ecosystems of endemic flora and fauna were fighting to come back to life, although sadly, these places will take many decades to thrive again.

The substrate of this regrowth is soil, the "living, breathing skin of the Earth."[1] It supports, in some way, nearly all life on earth's land surface and is, therefore, of critical importance for ecosystems and humanity. Bucak's exhibition is anchored by the immersive

1. William Bryant Logan, *Dirt: The Ecstatic Skin of the Earth* (New York: W. W. Norton & Company, 2007)

installation *Numbing silence covers us like fine dust* (2022), which uses a sculptural gesture of geographic transference to draw attention to soil desertification after high-intensity wildfires. While some fires can be beneficial for soil, high-intensity fires such as the ones in 2021 destroy soil's nutrients, impeding the regeneration of the land.[2] For this work, the artist visited forests in Tunceli, a Kurdish-Alevi majority province in Eastern Anatolia, after they had been decimated by the 2021 wildfires. This area has a long history of environmental destruction due to the prolonged and violent conflict between the Turkish army and the Kurdistan Workers' Party (PKK): the Turkish army systematically burned forests to destroy the PKK militants' hideouts. While traveling in the region, Bucak gathered ashes and soil for the installation, which is more than 3.5 meters tall and 14 meters wide, reminiscent of a cutout slice of a mountain. This environment in the gallery space simultaneously activates the viewer's senses of smell, sight, and sound, bringing a complex geography thousands of kilometers away to Dresden. Along with the collected earth, Bucak recorded the sound of the unproductive soil throughout the area, with microphones submerged underground to pick up the sounds of emptiness

→ 1–4, 13–16

2. The ash produced by fires is full of nutrients and can help with soil restoration; in other words, dust can be a natural fertilizer. Moreover, high temperatures increase dust production.

that reverberate through barren land. These recordings were then amplified and incorporated into a minimal composition enveloping the entire installation space, actualizing the chilling silence and lifelessness that permeates burned forests.

Throughout the months of the exhibition, *Numbing silence covers us like fine dust* functioned as a platform for a durational performance. *The gift of sight* (2022) took place on, in, and around the installation through improvised actions by → 94–97 a solo dancer. The installation's arid landscape was kicked up by the motions of the dancer, who became smeared in dust from writhing, clenching, sitting, and standing on top of the installation, meters above the viewer. In moments of stillness and motion, the performance (which lasted approximately ten minutes) contemplated resistance and the displacement of people due to conflict and ecological devastation. In a testament to the wildfires that spurred the work's existence, the dancer seemingly grew out of ashes in an act of perseverance.

Similarly, *A tree* (2022), a 12-panel mosaic → 33–39 assembled from thousands of burned organic remnants from the forest fires, rose from the wildfire's dust. For this this new work, the artist collected tree branches, bones, ashes, metal, and stones by hand during walks in forests in Turkey, creating a tree "composed from its ashes." In this sense, the work is made from a catastrophic event of unmaking. Even though the fires dulled the forest's luminosity, the pieces Bucak collected are not achromatic; their gold, orange, red, and blue hues are tightly constructed together to show that life follows death. Building on the ancient cultural tradition of mosaics by using broken and closely set pieces (historically, stone and glass) to form an image, *A tree* points to both the centuries-long growth of its materials and the mere hours it took to destroy them. The artist gathered the materials in *A tree* from areas in Eastern Anatolia that have significant political relevance, where the fires lasted for weeks. In this region, forest fires are politically charged events, whether natural or instigated by individuals, and so *A tree* is born from the state violence that detriments the environment.

→ 77–85

*They burned it all* (2022) is also based on Bucak's fieldwork in several wildfire sites. This video installation brings together two performances: the first enacted by the artist herself in a charred forest landscape, and the second performed by five pairs of singers in a municipal theater in Istanbul. The synchronous videos highlight the essential role of listening and speaking in healing. As the artist slowly crawls along the blackened terrain, she listens intently into the earth, now devoid of life. This endless loop of her journey is interjected by a singer who cannot make an utterance; she is silenced. At the same time, the singer and the other nine members of her choir prepare for a performance. Nevertheless, as it begins, they are motionless on stage, staring ahead with total concentration as though suspended in time. Although they are unable to sing it themselves, they hear their song. It interprets the phrase "they burned it all" into a lament. However, they sing each letter alone in a broken sentence in Kurdish—a language not heard in most theaters in Turkey. And so we hear "*Her tişt şewitandin*," letter by letter.

Burning language as an act of political violence is the subject of *Black Ink* (2019), a typographic print made with ink from a burned book's ashes. Created with movable type, this textual print documents the recipe for the ink used to print its letters. Its recipe states, "... Then black ash taken from a book burned on June 10, 2016 in Diyarbakır was added. The ash was steadily mixed into the solution over several hours to create a paste of uniform consistency... A measure of soot from a razed house was added to the book ash to

→ 63, 65–67

deepen the color." The recipe unveils the tragic events of its origin—ashes from a burned Kurdish book and a wrecked house were added to a solution to create the ink. The Kurdish language has been long persecuted in Turkey, and *Black Ink* bears witness to the burning of a Kurdish publishing house in Diyarbakır, a city in southeast Turkey. Alas, fires have been deliberately incited throughout history to destroy cultural heritage and memory, as is the case for the fire at the center of *Black Ink*.

→ 86, 91–93

For *Hate to disturb this precious silence* (2021), the artist collected a cast-off piece of timber from an urban construction site. In the subsequent four-channel video performance, she sits in her studio for hours, cradling and repeatedly sanding away the roughness of the wood. The sound of the sanding is like a mantra that aids her concentration as she carefully and gradually removes surface debris and uneven wood parts. It is as though she is healing the plank by undoing the damage it sustained and its separation from the forest. The work meditates on humanity's profound connection to nature and the precarity of living on a planet critically threatened by environmental destruction and climate change. This sense of uncertainty extends to the accompanying composition, integrating the sanding sounds into a musical score.

As a "living" exhibition that develops over months in Dresden, *While the Dust Quickly Falls* includes *An interlude* (2022), a garden archive in a gallery-cum-greenhouse. Assembled by the artist in collaboration with a medical plant specialist, the installation features more than a hundred plants used throughout history for distinctly dual purposes: in small amounts for healing human illnesses and injuries, and in large amounts as toxic substances that can induce harm. Many of the plants have been used since ancient times for these purposes. The 17 species—poppy, wormwood, foxglove, ivy, sea onion, tobacco, sage, oleander, and nutmeg among them—are illuminated by grow lights and sit on industrial shelves. Used widely in workspaces such as garden sheds, laboratories, and libraries, these shelves shelter the plants that cascade over them. The plant's medicinal usages range from narcotics to tonics, sedatives, anti-asthmatics, stimulants, analgesics, expectorants, laxatives, digestives, and anti-inflammatories. Equally wide-ranging are the plant's origins: they are found on five of the seven continents (not Australia and Antarctica). During the exhibition, this garden grows thanks to care from the Kunsthaus Dresden staff, providing moments of pause from the everyday and a space

→ 26–27, 99–111

of metaphorical healing for visitors, connecting to the critical need to conserve and protect species for the health of the planet and humanity. [2]

*An interlude* continues Bucak's interest in embedding the survival of nature into her work. In 2016, she initiated *Damascus rose* (2016–ongoing), a long-term project that attempts to recultivate the Damask rose, a much-loved and once ubiquitous rose species found in Syria. Due to the continuing Syrian civil war, many of the Damask rose fields in the country have been abandoned. In 2016, the artist read that their production had decreased by 70 percent, and she initiated the *Damascus rose* project to recultivate them. Beginning with an arduous journey in which Bucak "smuggled" more than a hundred Damask roses out of Syria, the roses traveled thousands of kilometers as branches without roots, with the help of many people along the way. She then grafted them onto local rose species in the cities where they were exhibited and planted them in flower beds to grow in exhibitions. Bucak's Damask roses have been shown in various configurations and quantities in art institutions across the globe. Nurtured by the staff of each exhibiting institution, some have grown better than others. A few of these Damask roses were planted inside pots at the Kunsthaus

→ 43–48

3. The plants from this work were transferred after the exhibition to the garden branch of the Kunsthaus Dresden, where they form a permanent archive and healing garden.

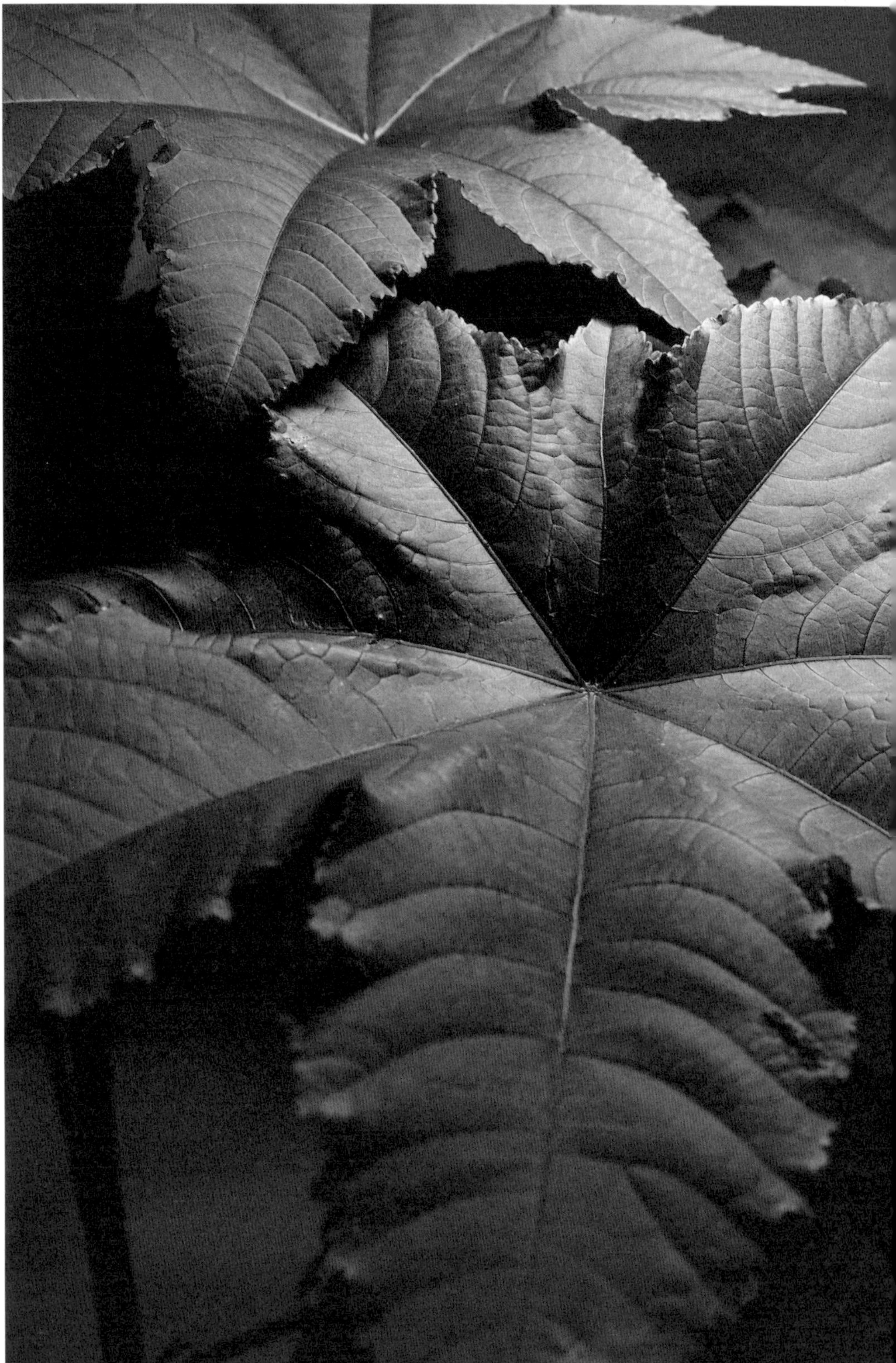

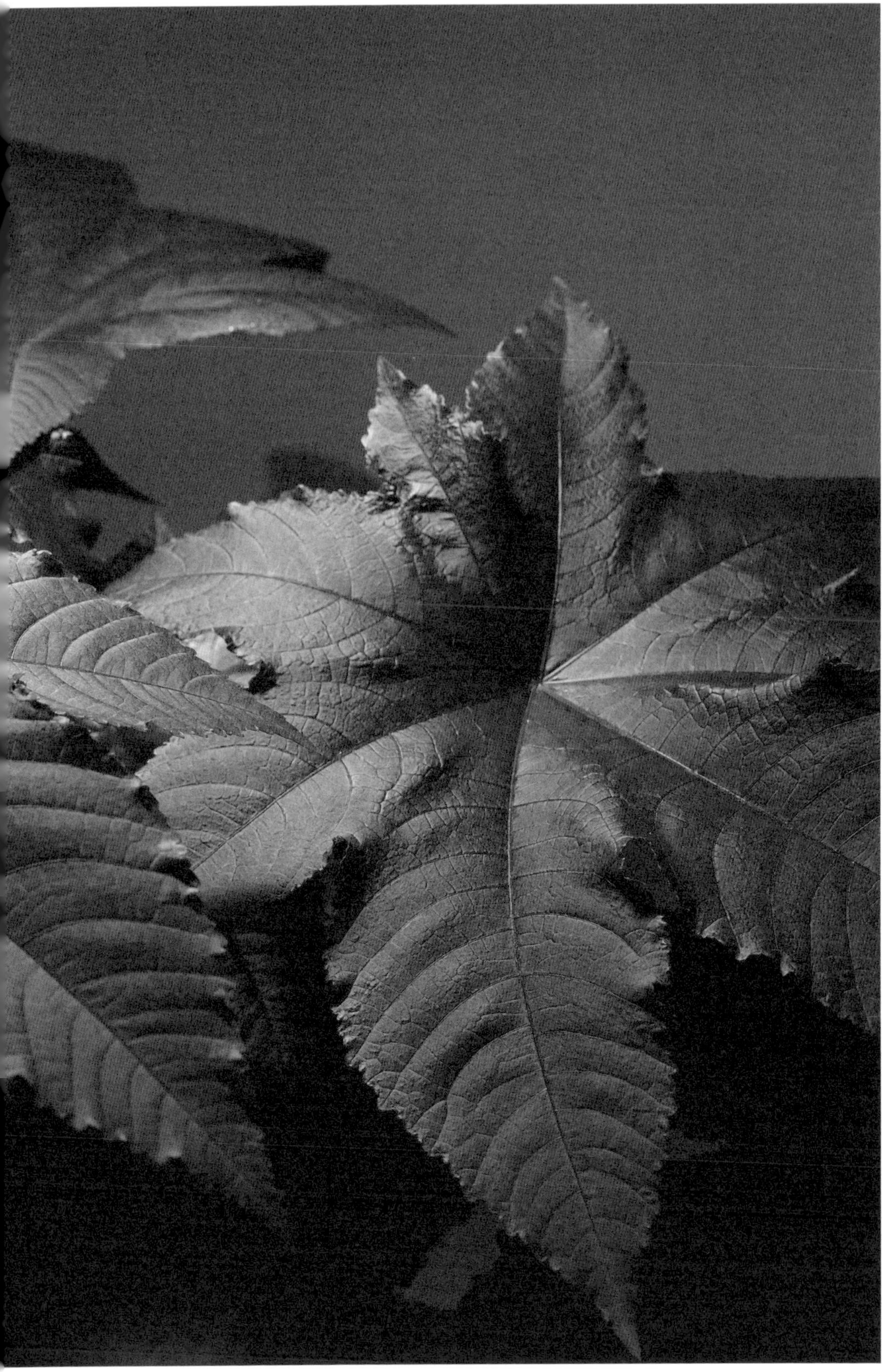

Dresden, where they bloom and prosper. The *Damascus rose* project builds upon central ideas present throughout the artist's practice: borders, trauma, the displacement of people, and memory.

Often, non-human animals are also displaced due to war and climate change. *Sum of the misdeeds and consents and cowardly acts* (2022) is an installation of ten bronze birds inhabiting Iraq. The International Union for Conservation of Nature's Red List of Threatened Species has designated all the represented birds as vulnerable, endangered, or critically endangered. This list accounts for the health of the world's biodiversity and is also an essential resource for conservationists. Some of the birds in the installation rely on Iraq's marshlands, and the drainage of these areas over decades for political reasons has severely compromised their habitats. All the birds are cast in resting poses and in different sizes and weights; the largest/heaviest is the most critically endangered, while the smallest/lightest is the least endangered or vulnerable, according to the Red List. The slender-billed curlew, sociable lapwing, Basra reed warbler, steppe eagle, white-headed duck, saker falcon, MacQueen's bustard, greater spotted eagle, marbled duck, and

→ 112–119

common pochard are lined up in the installation according to their ranking on the Red List.

The birds are installed on a pedestal covered with a Middle Eastern folk textile. They are conceptually based on a Mesopotamian weight shaped like a bird that was part of the National Museum of Iraq's collection until it was looted during the Iraq War two decades ago. To date, it is unrecovered. Ancient weights were not only measuring instruments but also emblems of power. Connecting endangered birds to these weights implies systems of control and value; humankind used weights for trade to determine the worth of commodities. In this sense, *Sum of the misdeeds and consents and cowardly acts* asks: What is the value of non-human life in already troubled territories?

Conservation efforts are often thwarted by conflict or its constant imminence. Each of the 350 screen prints delicately crafted into stone-like sculptures in *Perpetual lure and insistent fear* (2022) represents one of the remaining wildflowers of the Golan iris (*Iris hermona*).
→ 120–126
These endangered irises grow almost exclusively in the Golan Heights, a militarized zone where tank exercises and settlements have impacted their habitat. Furthermore, climate change, cattle grazing, and expanding vineyards have

decreased their populations. Many of the irises that still exist are in minefields. Bucak has reimagined the Golan iris's deep purple veins, brown spots, and underlying white and lilac colors. She presents them in the exhibition as a field with colors that do not adhere to reality: crimson reds, sharp yellows, indigo blues, and verdant greens. *Perpetual lure and insistent fear* makes the irises proliferate again in an accessible place, the Kunsthaus Dresden. They take the form of stones as a reminder of their natural environs, where they grow in rocky basalt soil. Yet, they are not heavy. As fragile paper stones, they remind us, in the artist's words, "how nature, although strong, can no longer heal itself."

What comes after its destruction if nature can no longer heal itself? Human activities are constantly reshaping the earth, and biodiversity loss is inequitable. Communities—particularly those disenfranchised by their states—become more precarious as their habitats become more and more fragile. *While the Dust Quickly Falls* traces the state's deep footprints on the environmental crisis, from deforestation, species extinction, biodiversity loss, droughts, and climate change. In its reflection on the profound loss and mourning of ecosystems—ecological grief—the exhibition opens a space for action and hope.

Postscript: The 2021 fires were the most widespread in Turkey's history, with more than 150,000 hectares of land burned, hastened by the state's unpreparedness and negligence. On February 6, 2023, a series of earthquakes hit southern and central Turkey and northwestern Syria. The deadliest in Turkey's modern history, they reduced entire towns and cities to rubble—and dust. The state's absolute failure to respond to the catastrophe was further amplified when the authorities systematically undermined civil society's efforts to help, even limiting internet use in the earthquake zone.

*Kari Conte is a curator and writer based in New York City and Yalıkavak, Turkey. She is the curator of* While the Dust Quickly Falls.

p. 33–39:

***A tree***, 2022
Mosaic made from diverse burned forest materials collected during the 2021 fires in Eastern Anatolia and other areas in Southern Turkey
152 × 200 cm

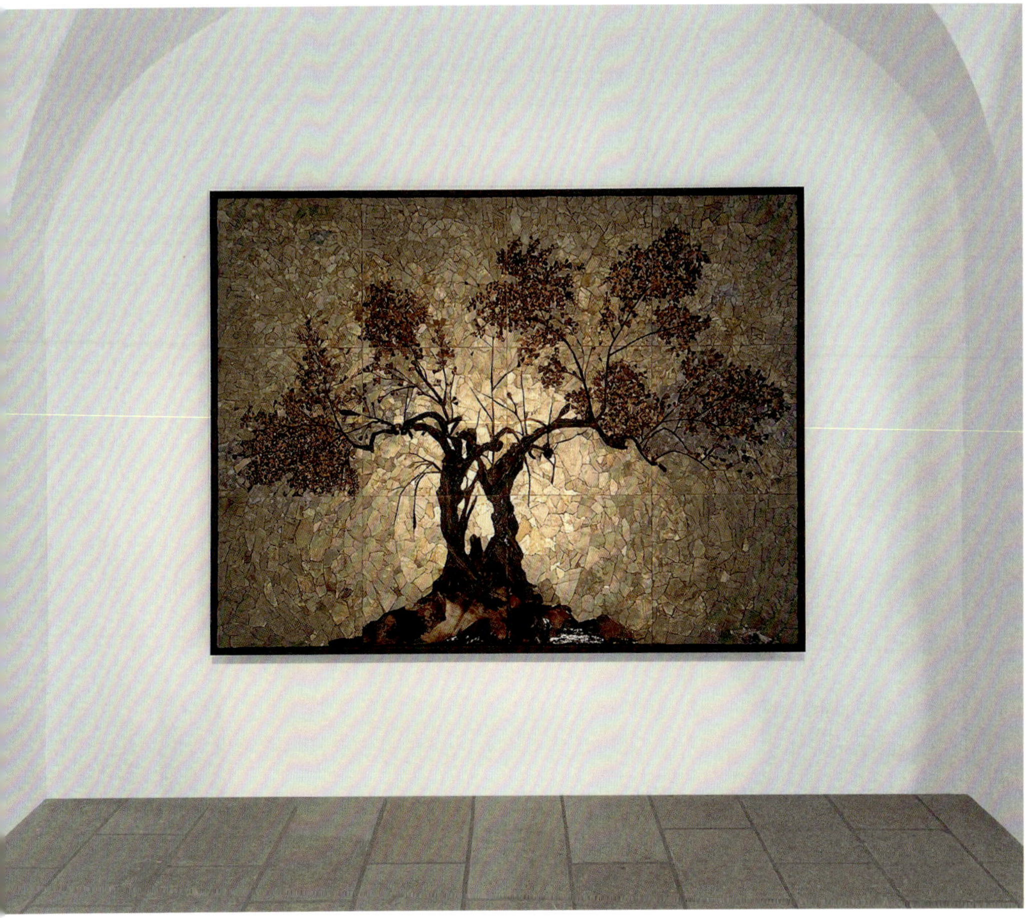

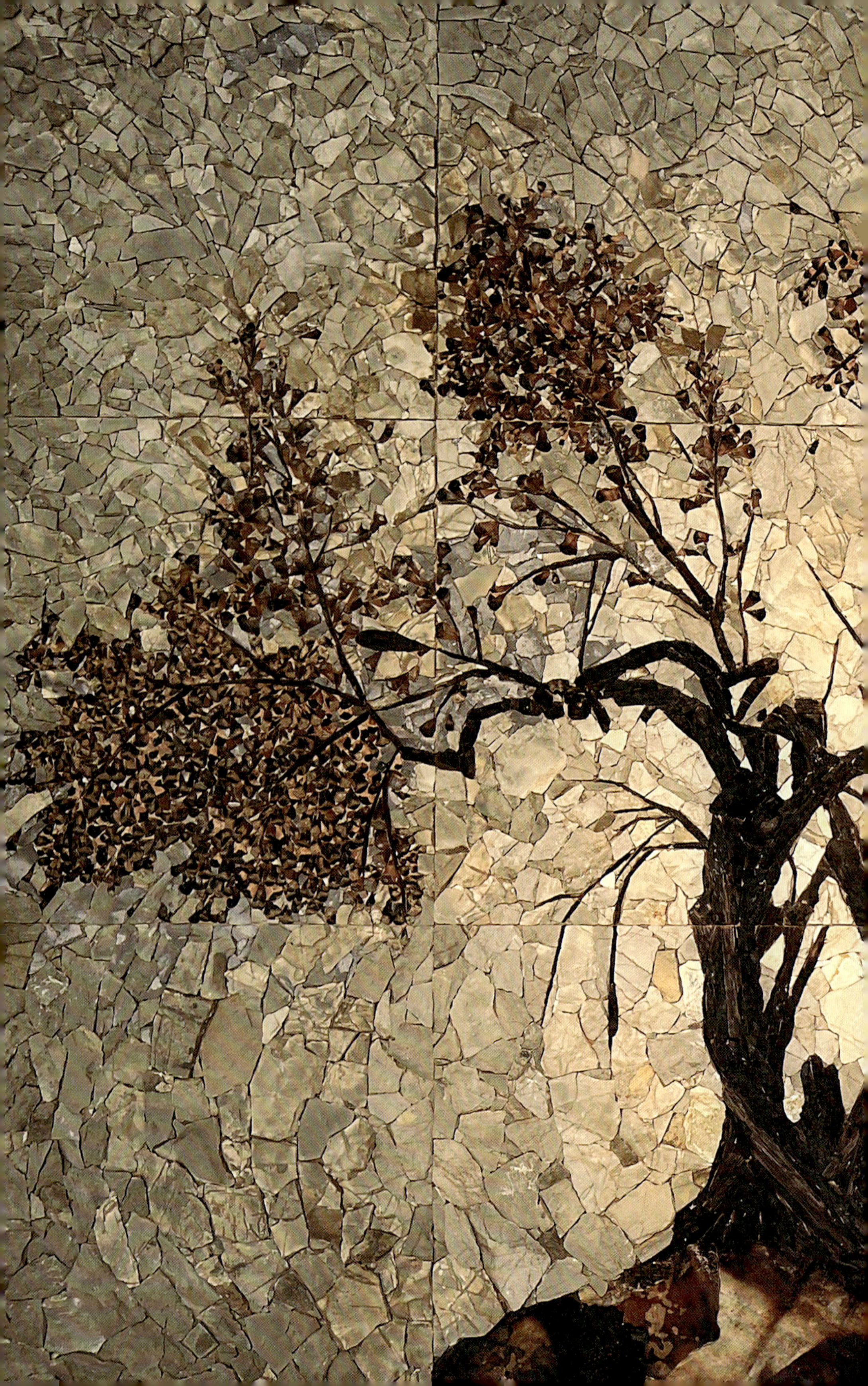

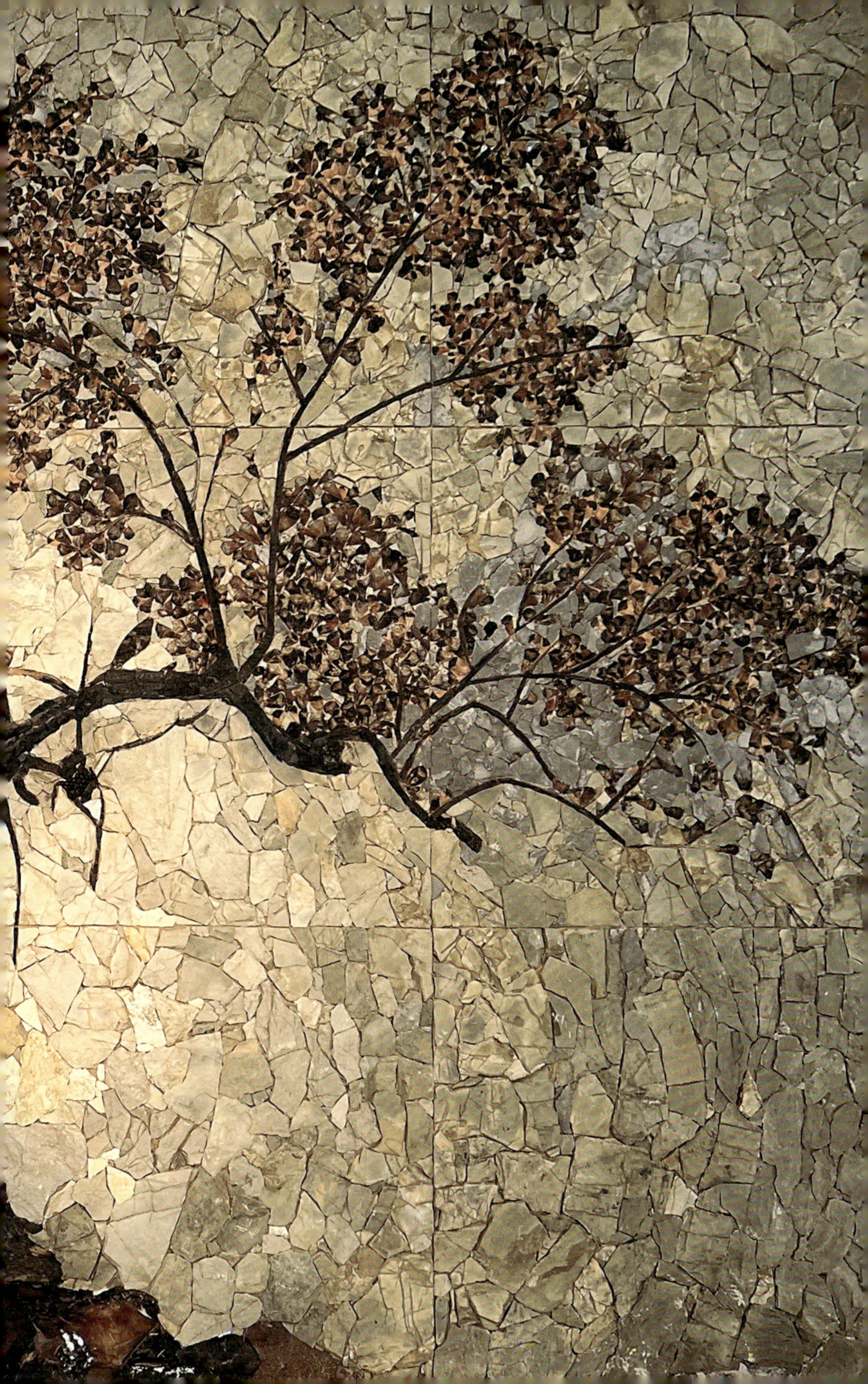

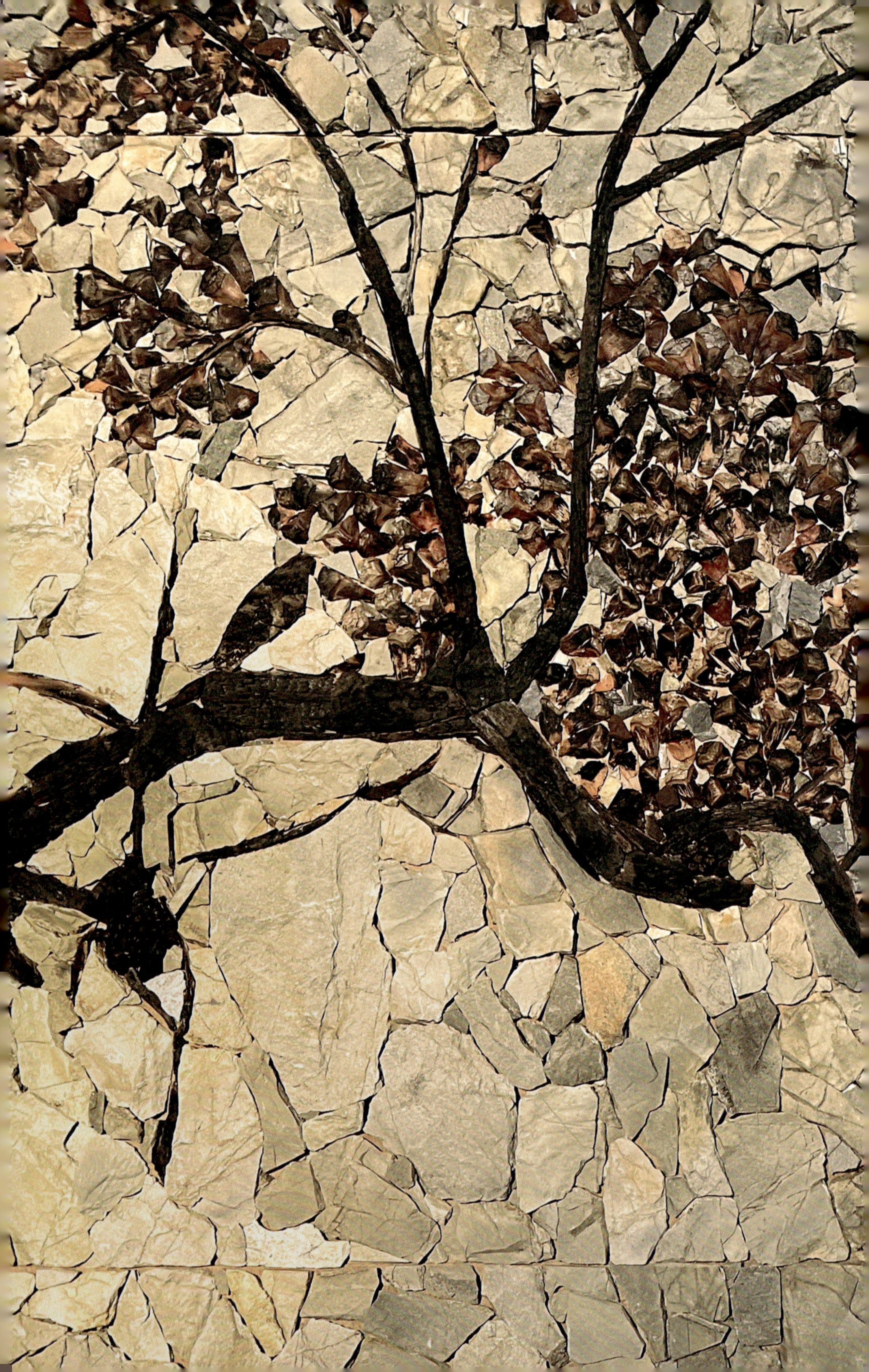

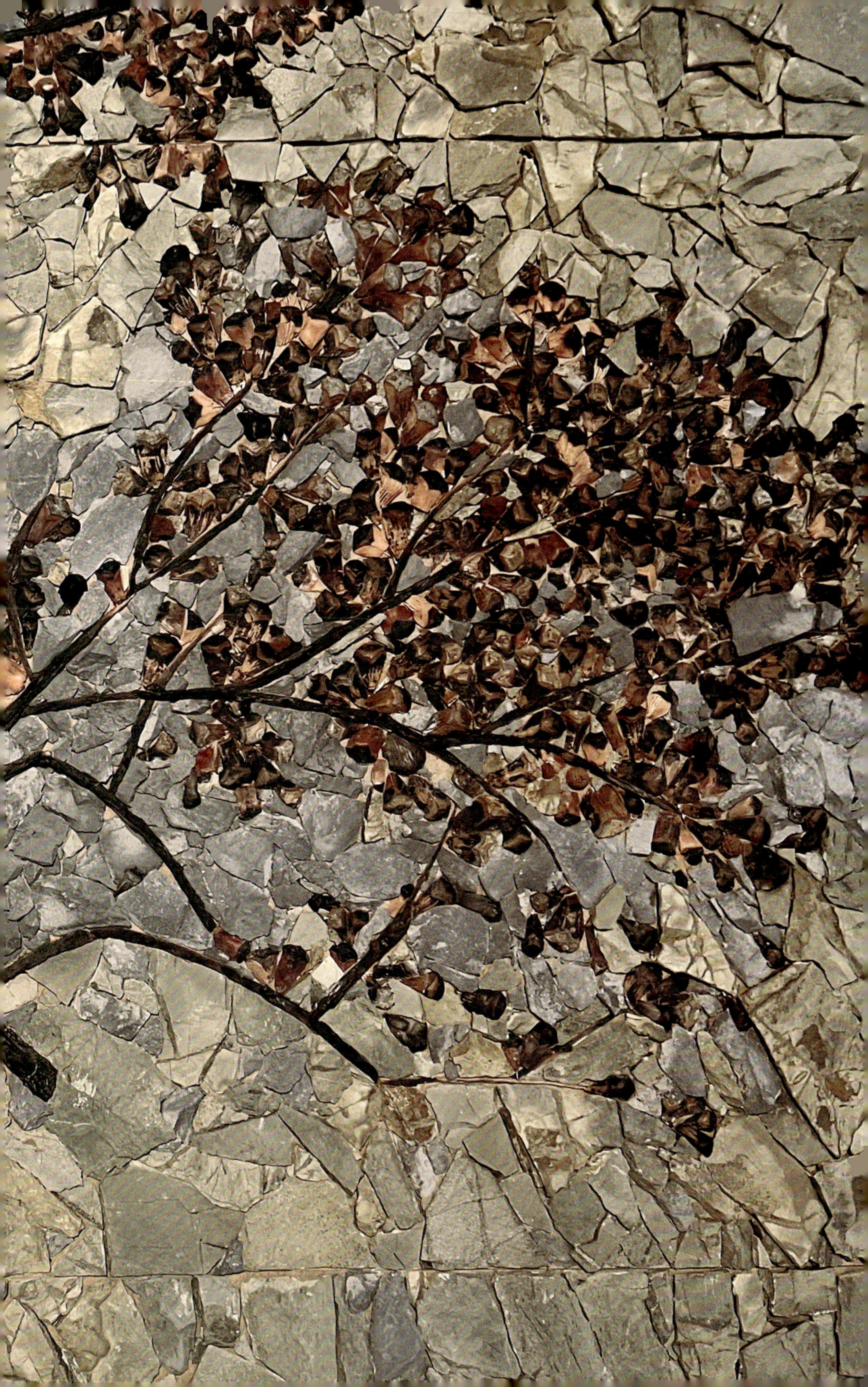

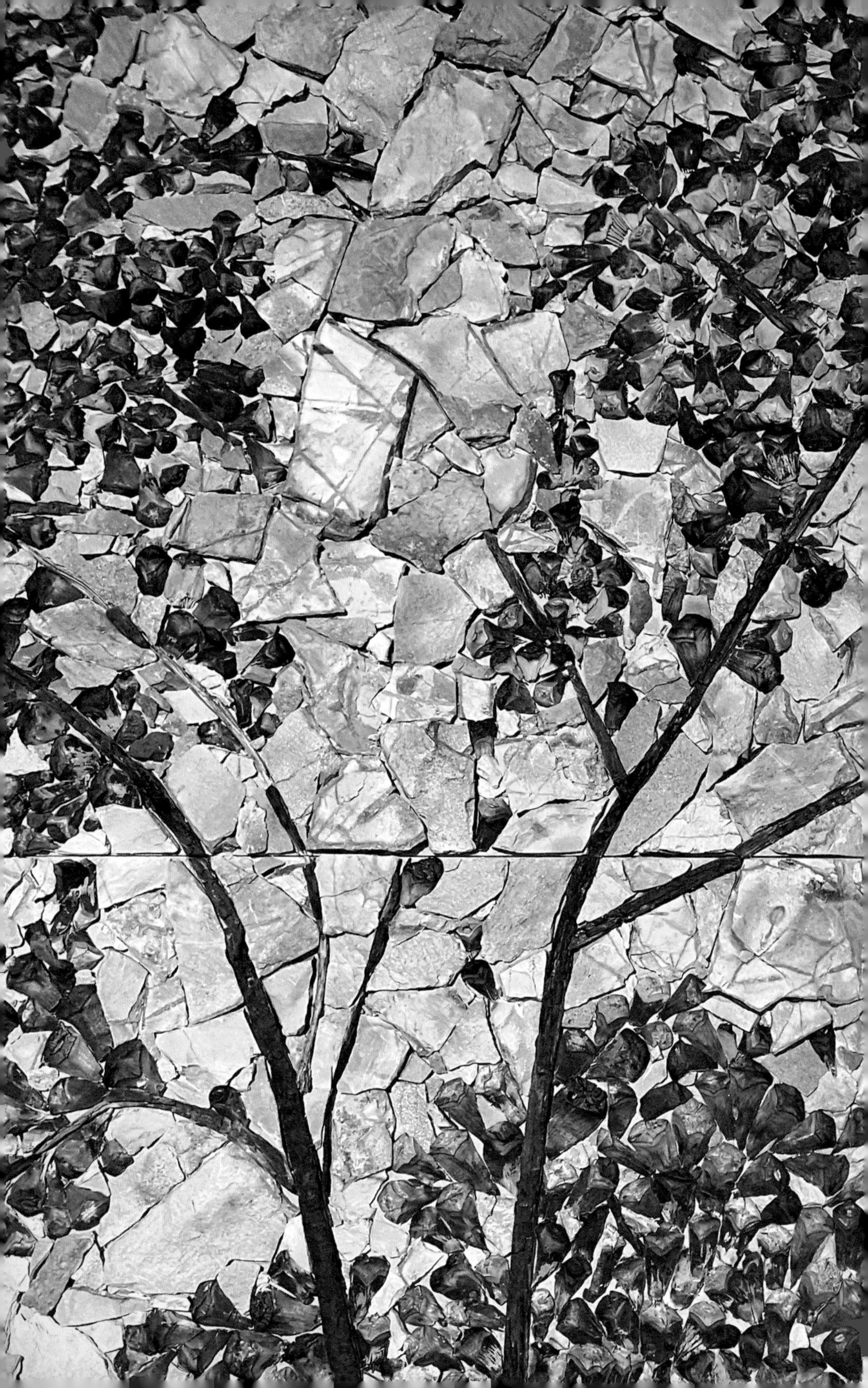

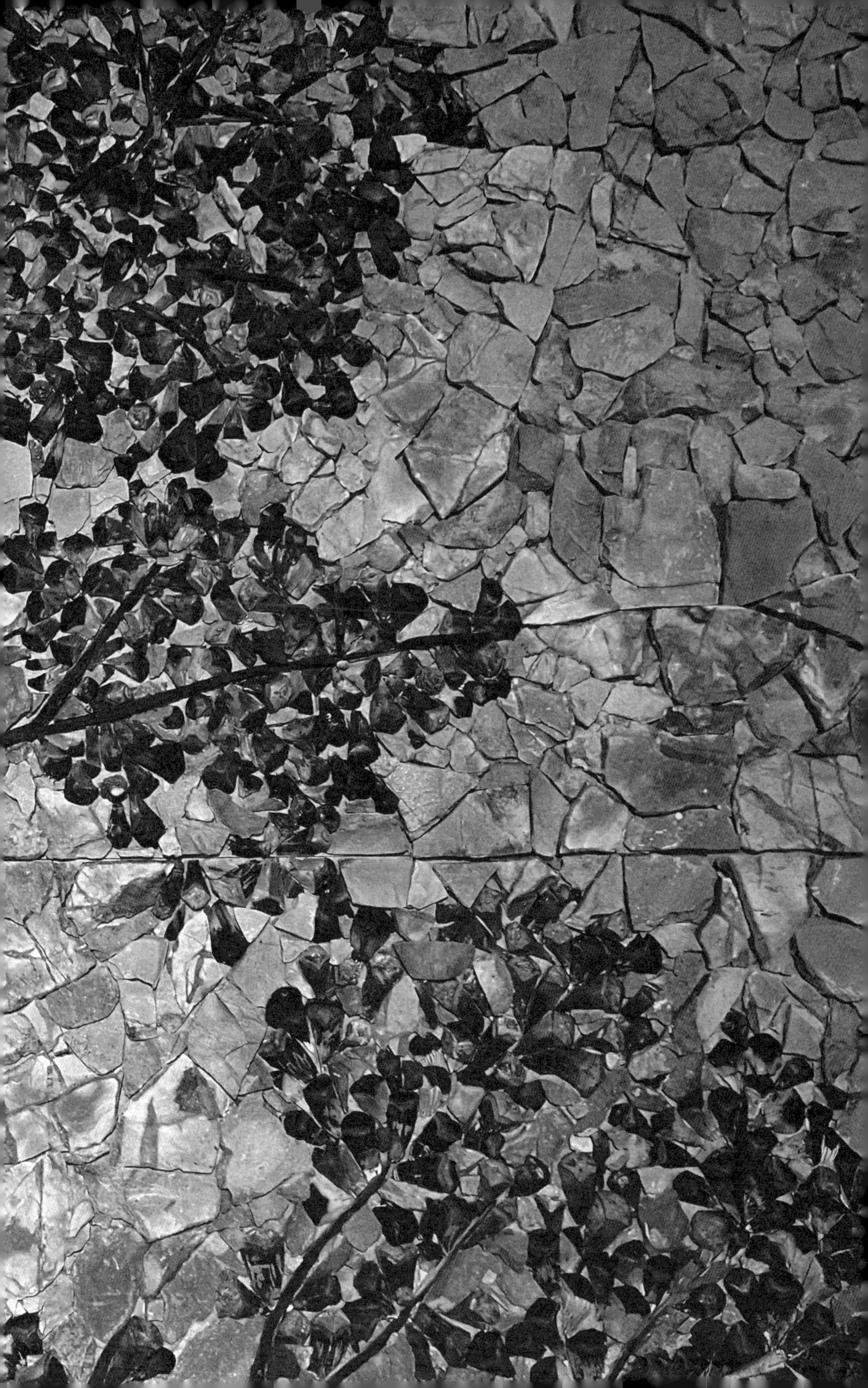

*the dust that*

*a bombing, th*

*the deliberate*

*associated w*

*the dust of ra*

*wildfires, the*

*impossible to*

*insistently ac*

*ppears after*
*dust from*
*urning*
*n conflict,*
*ging*
*st, almost*
*rush off and*
*mulating...*

p. 43–48:

***Damascus rose***, 2016–ongoing
Damask roses grown from grafted rose cuttings from Damascus, Syria
Dimensions variable
Project realized with the support of the Italian Council (2022)

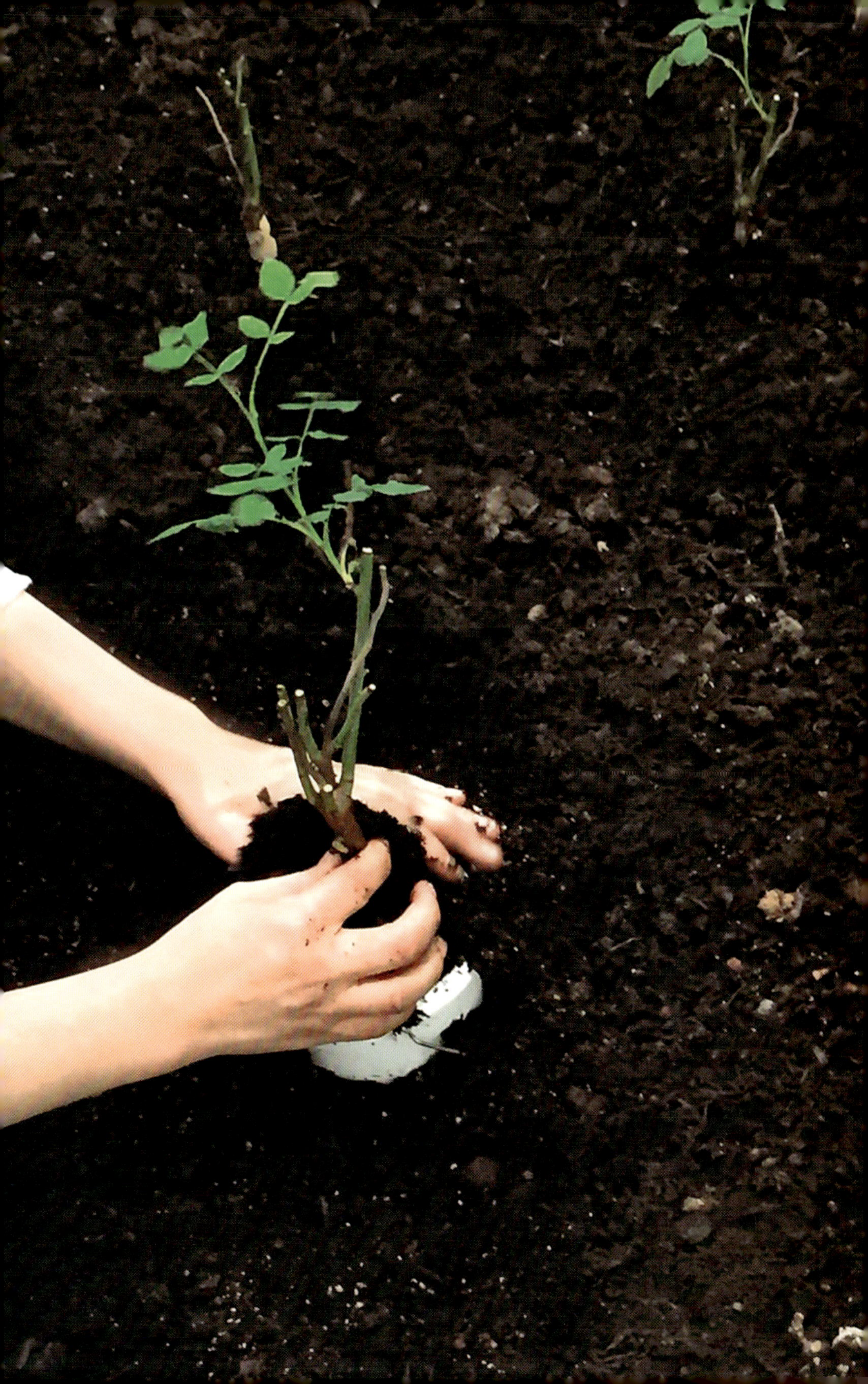

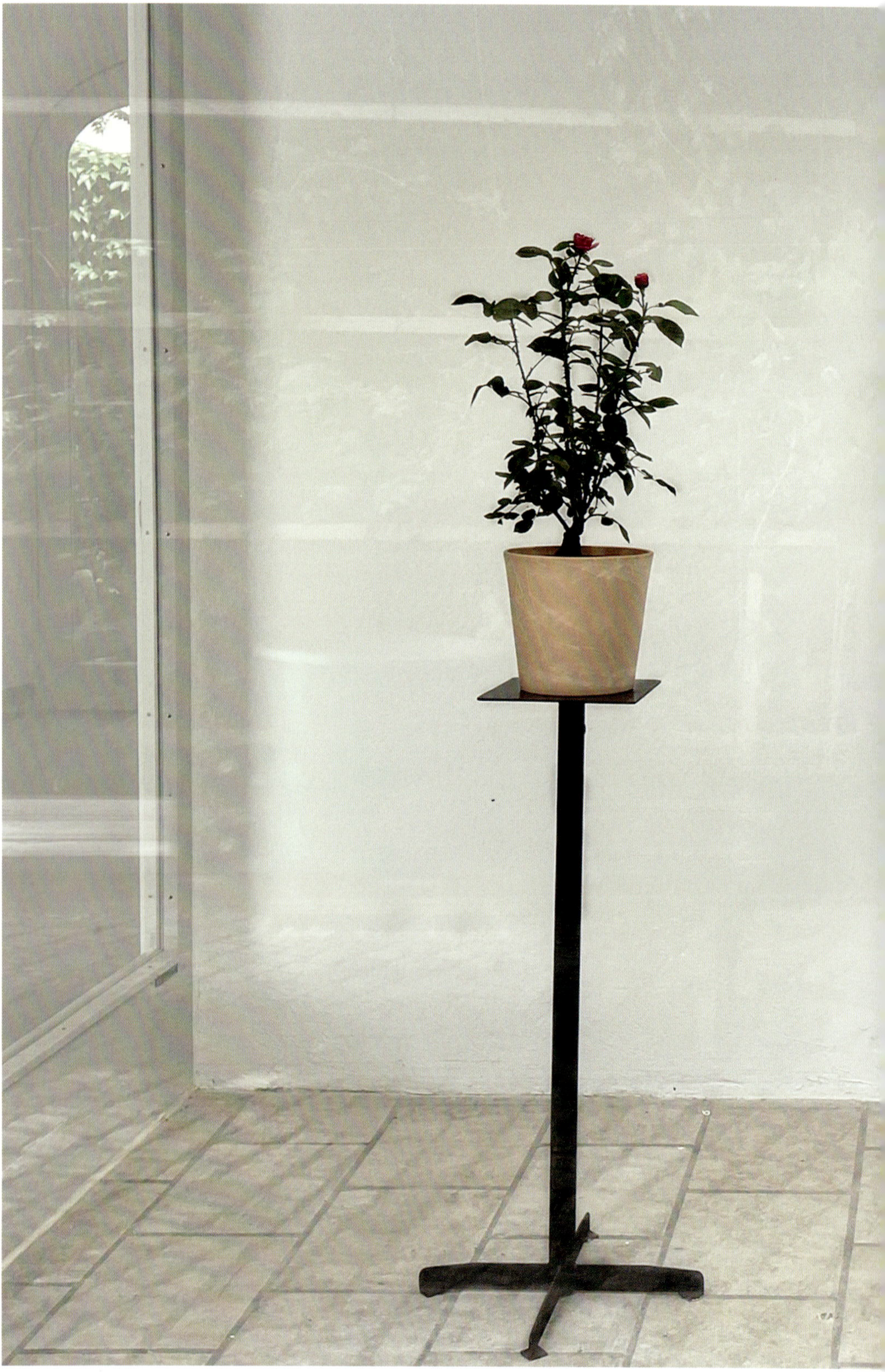

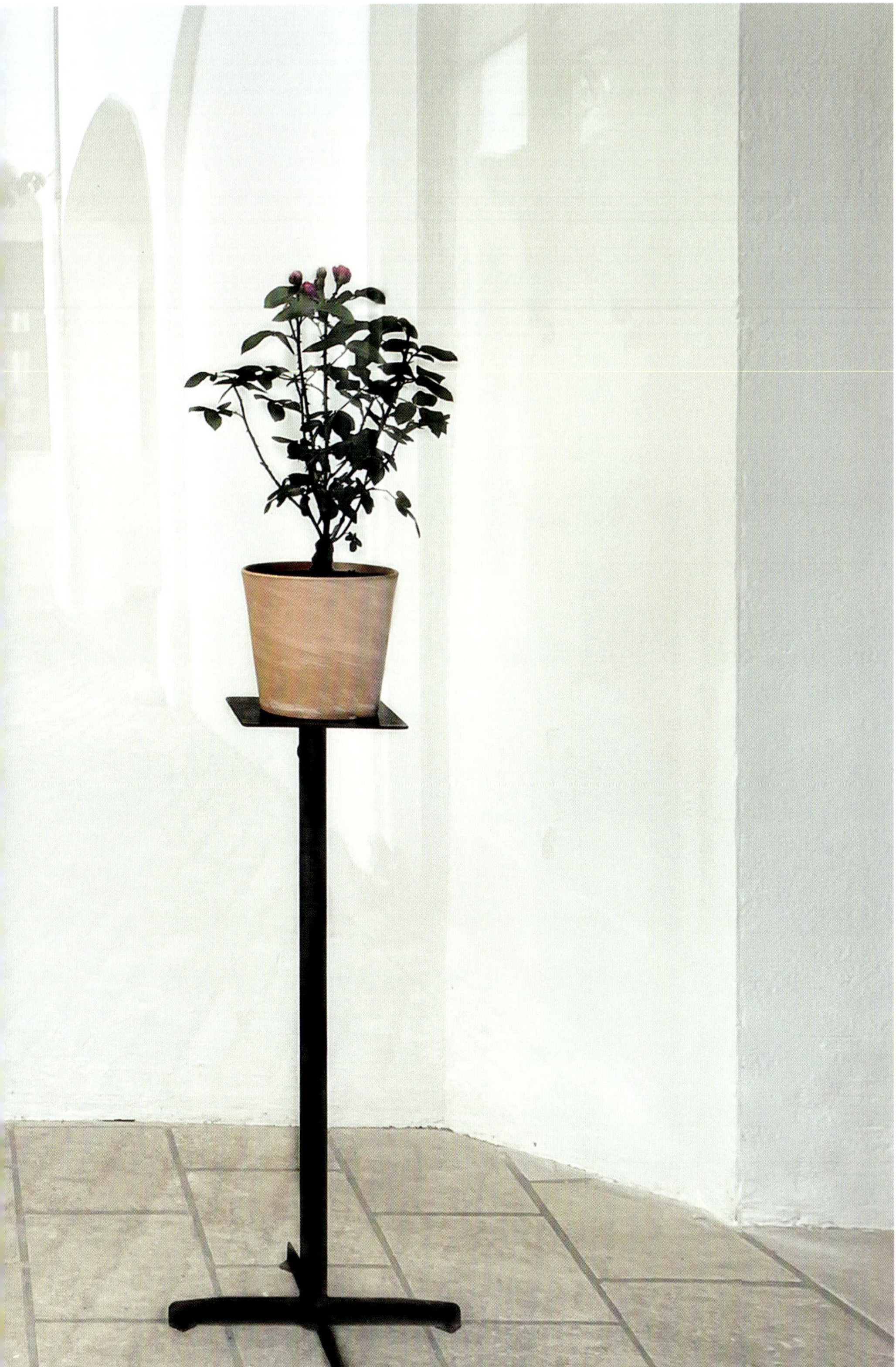

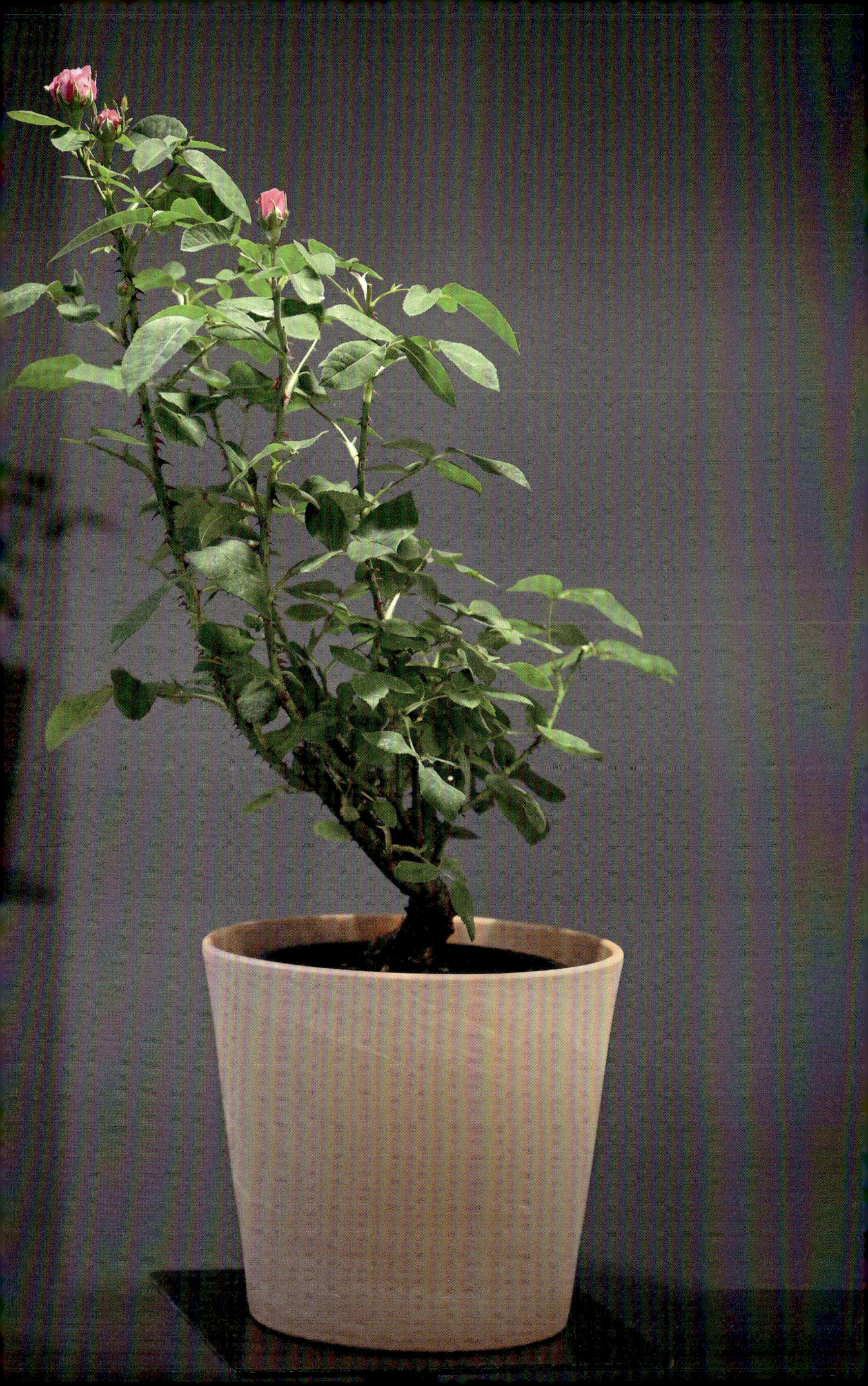

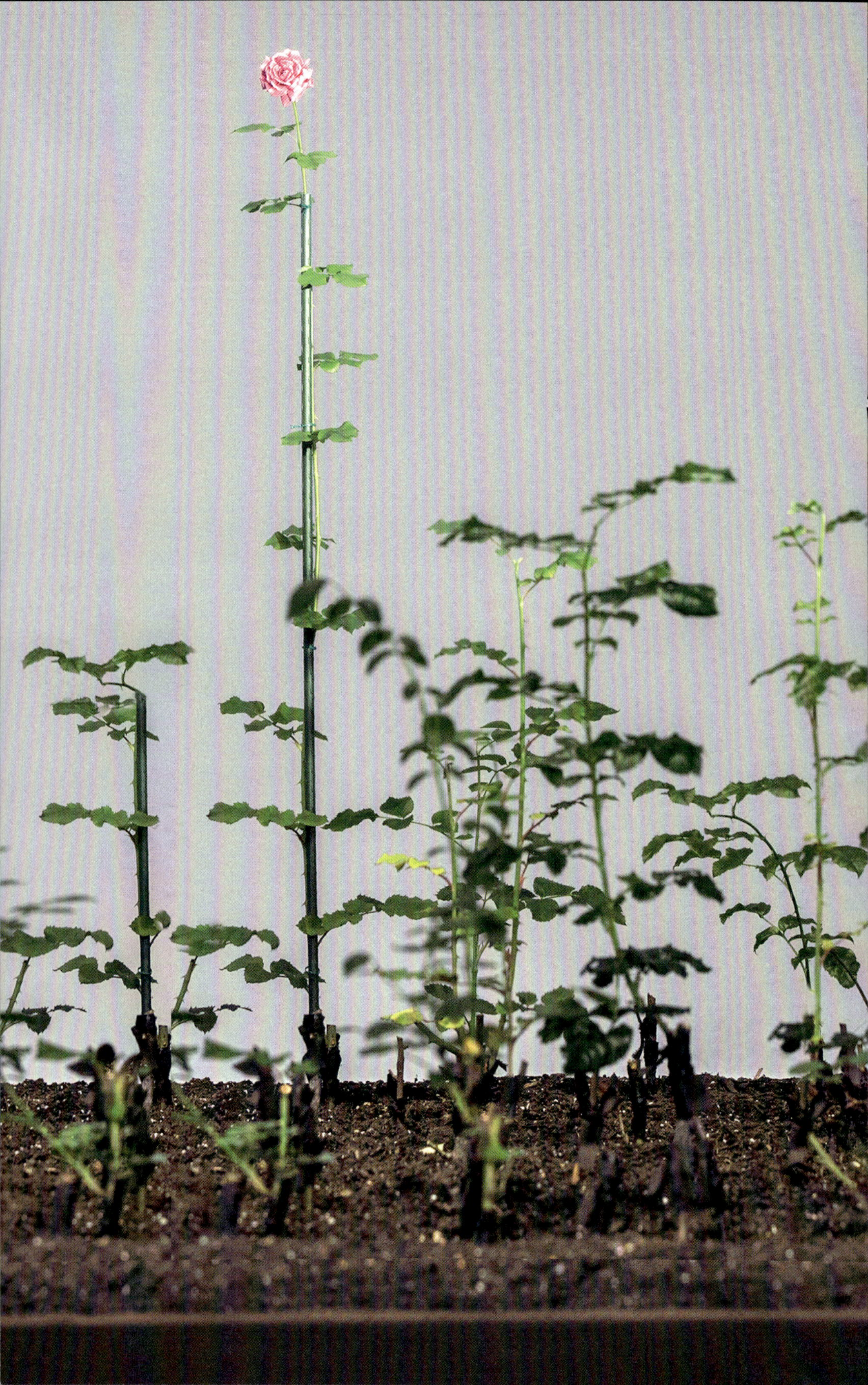

# Dustwork

ERAY ÇAYLI

Dust interweaves various materialities in *While the Dust Quickly Falls*—ashes (whether of burned forests or books), sawdust, and granular soil—imbricating current ecologies in Fatma Bucak's native Turkey and its environs with histories of political violence. The present is a historical juncture where the links between climate change and violent histories are increasingly salient and the subject of intense debate. Is climate change simply a case of what victims of violent political projects have long experienced—now unfolding on a planetary scale and in increasingly spectacular ways? Or do its effects on places and communities marginalized due to violent histories remain disproportionate? If longstanding violent political projects are the crux of the matter, what distinguishes the current juncture in the progress climate change? These questions indicate ever-growing tensions along such axes as the particular versus the universal, the local versus the planetary, and the processual versus the spectacular. I wish to ask how an aesthetic and political focus on dust might address these tensions.

## The Spectacularity of Dust

Dust is increasingly spectacular in today's Turkey. Dune-like piles of sand appear in quarries or outside construction sites, aerial footage of burned-down forests visualizes landscapes entirely made up of ash, and desert storms from Iraq and Syria cloud urban skies. Indeed, all these examples are interlinked, and violence runs through this interlinkage.

Sandpiles relate to the construction sector and one of the extractive industries that feeds it: sand mining. The construction sector has become increasingly central to Turkey's economic model since the country's integration into global neoliberal markets in the 1980s. This integration was enforced violently by the military coup of September 12, 1980, at the expense of thousands of killed, maimed, disappeared, and imprisoned counter-establishment politicians, revolutionary activists, and Kurds. Turkey's reliance on the construction sector reached unprecedented heights after 2012, when the parliament passed a piece of legislation dubbed the Disaster Law. The law has unleashed a series of "urban transformation" projects with the aim of disaster-proofing Turkey's building stock. But, in effect, it has instrumentalized the sacrosanct cause of disaster resilience by rendering construction and redevelopment activity incontestable.[1] The law has been implemented for knocking down and

1. Eray Çaylı, "Introduction: The material and spatial politics of emergency," in Eray Çaylı, Pınar Aykac and Sevcan Ercan, eds., *Architectures of Emergency in Turkey: Heritage, Displacement and Catastrophe* (London: Bloomsbury/IB Tauris, 2021), 1–20.

rebuilding entire neighborhoods, including self-built, working-class, and often-racialized ones known as *gecekondu*, which were once in the urban periphery but now find themselves on lucrative land.

In most cases, the redevelopment of *gecekondu* neighborhoods pushes residents out to the new metropolitan periphery, exacerbating already existing marginalization and urban sprawl. Neighborhoods redeveloped as such are exploited not only for their exchange value but also for their use value. The rubble used to create the 100-hectare Orhangazi Coastal Park in the Istanbul district of Maltepe through land reclamation came from *gecekondu* neighborhoods demolished for redevelopment.[2] Marginalized communities are also affected by the construction sector's precarious and unsafe working conditions as they constitute much of its labor force. Those who had fled theaters of imperial warfare such as Syria and Afghanistan now figure increasingly prominently in this labor force, a continuation on from earlier decades when the construction sector relied heavily on Kurds displaced by the war between state forces and Kurdish guerrillas in Turkey's Kurdistan. The construction sector, then, originates in, reproduces, and benefits from histories of political violence.

The sandpiles' spectacular dustiness is linked to forest fires and desert storms. Some of the fires are caused by arsonists aiming to make land

2. Elvan Kıvılcım, "Gecekondu molozları üzerinde emek bayramı," *1+1 Express*, April 29, 2018, https://birartibir.org/gecekondu-molozlari-uzerinde-emek-bayrami/; MO İstanbul, "Basına ve Kamuoyuna Zorunlu Açıklama: Maltepe Dolgu Alanı Miting Alanı Değil, Bir Kent Suçudur," TMMOB Mimarlar Odası İstanbul Büyükkent Şubesi, April 29, 2018, www.mimarist.org/basina-ve-kamuoyuna-zorunlu-aciklama-maltepe-dolgu-alani-miting-alani-degil-bir-kent-sucudur.

available for construction activity.[3] Most result from the summer heat that is becoming increasingly scorching due to climate change, one of whose chief drivers in Turkey is the construction sector—the continuous extraction it requires and the greenfield development it causes. The construction sector's relation to desert storms is less straightforward than its role in forest fires and therefore requires further detail. The extractive industries that feed the construction sector are implicated in the desert storms that arrived in 2021 from Syria and Iraq to cities in Turkey, a seasonal event that now comes "far earlier" in the year "than normal" and affects "a much wider area."[4] The chief causes of these changes include desertification, especially around the Tigris and the Euphrates, a process driven significantly by Turkey's extensive damming of these rivers.[5]

The dams are entangled in a history of colonial violence where European powers first constructed the "Middle East" as such and then partitioned it into nation-states, with each resulting nation-state oppressing its minoritized communities, notably the Kurds, who remain stateless and separated by the borders between Turkey, Iraq, Syria, and Iran. In 1990, as construction of the first two dams built on the Tigris had just started, the Turkish parliament amended its Coast Law banning construction activity on Turkey's seashores and the banks of its major rivers, including

3. Tolga Güney, "Orman yangınlarının altından rant ve talan çıkıyor," *Mezopotamya Ajansı*, June 28, 2022, http://mezopotamyaajansi35.com/tum-haberler/content/view/175628.

4. Richa Syal, "'Apocalyptic skies': the dust storms devastating Gulf states and Syria," The Guardian, June 3, 2022, https://www.theguardian.com/environment/2022/jun/03/apocalyptic-skies-dust-storms-wreaking-havoc-iraq-syria. According to the UN, "between 1951–1990, there were an average of 24 days per year with dust storms in Iraq, compared to 122 in 2013." See "Iraq's perfect storm – a climate and environmental crisis amid the scars of war," International Committee of the Red Cross, July 19, 2021, https://www.icrc.org/en/document/iraqs-perfect-storm-climate-and-environmental-crisis-amid-scars-war.

5. "Briefing: Climate Change in Iraq: Iraqis Are Facing an Existential Threat," Enabling Peace in Iraq Center (EPIC), September 23, 2022, https://enablingpeace.org/climate-briefing.

the Tigris. The amendment decreed that the Tigris begins about 100 kilometers downstream of what has been historically considered its origin and where the two dams were being built. The sociocultural and political heart of Turkey's Kurdistan, the city of Amed (in Turkish: Diyarbakır), is situated halfway along this stretch. The amendment's annulment of the river starting in the uppermost Tigris, coupled with Amed's intense construction activity throughout the 2000s and 2010s—not least to address the growing urban population of migrants fleeing war in the countryside—opened the riverbank to intense sand mining activity. More broadly, Turkey has long used its advantageous geolocation to stop waters from flowing downstream. It has leveraged them against Iraqi and Syrian administrations indifferent to Kurdish political movements headquartered in their territories. Turkey recently began using dam construction to create reservoirs that make the terrain impermeable to Kurdish guerrillas. The growing number and size of these reservoirs have caused a climatic impact, which is evident in the precipitation regime, including a decline in snowfall and an increase in unseasonal downpours. Both the clouds of sand that have recently filled the skies in Turkey and the piles of sand that continue to leap out of the country's quarries and construction sites, then, are intimately connected to the riverine wetness that dams have stopped from circulating—a circulation that has gone on for centuries.[6]

In today's extractivist-ridden and warming world, the spectacular quality of sandpiles, burned-down forests, and desert storms is indeed palpable in places other than just Turkey. When storms brought Saharan dust clouds to Western Europe in March 2022, spectacular orange-tinted photographs of cities dominated the news and social media posts.[7] News outlets are increasingly treating sand mining as a global problem by using photographs of sandpiles dwarfing individual humans.[8] The press covered recent wildfires in Australia and California with photographs of apocalyptic mushroom clouds and entire urban areas reduced to ash.[9] There is, then, a considerably universal character to dust's spectacularity today but one whose politics is not straightforward as it involves visual dialectics between translatability and homogenization. Working through these dialectics requires attending to dust's particularity, which lurks in its spectacular manifestations.

### The Particularity of Dust

Dust, by definition and in the most literal material sense, is particular: it consists of particles. Yet, this material particularity of dust is only sometimes considered carefully for its politics. Take some of the

6.
Eray Çaylı, "The Aesthetics of Extractivism: Violence, Ecology, and Sensibility in Turkey's Kurdistan," Antipode, vol. 53, 5 (2021): 1377–1399.

7.
Guillaume Woznica, "An impressive cloud of Sahara dust spreads over Western Europe," Your Weather, March 15, 2022, https://www.yourweather.co.uk/news trending/an-impressive-cloud-of-sahara-dust-spreads-over-western-europe-uk-spain-france.html. Some mainstream European press coverage of the previous year's dust storm (February 2021) emphasized that the event should not simply be seen as the stuff of orange-tinted spectacles. In fact, it carried to France the radiative residues of 1960s nuclear tests that the colonial power conducted in northern Africa. And so, the forme colony and the former metropole remain bound by extractivist relations as countries in the region continue to be plundered for resources for major European powers. See Samia Henni, "Oil, Gas, Dust: From the Sahara to Europe," e-flux Journal, October 8, 2021, https://www.e-flux.com/architecture/coloniality-infrastructure/410034/oil-gas-dust-from-the-sahara-to-europe.

examples mentioned above. For example, sandpiles accumulating in Amed's quarries are hard to ignore. They have even prompted the mainstream media to cover ecological destruction along the upper Tigris. This focus on the spectacularly political often overshadows the processual, inconspicuous, micro spatial politics of dust. In villages along the stretch of the upper Tigris where the river's riverness has been legislatively annulled to the effect of fuelling sand mining activity, different constituencies of villagers experience the dust differently. Men may complain about driving on roads damaged by earth-moving trucks or inhaling dusty air when walking around the village. But women, many of whom shoulder the unpaid labor of domestic work, speak of the grueling workload caused by the constant travel of dust from sand mines to their homes, making household cleanliness virtually impossible.[10] The case of the so-called urban transformation in Istanbul is no different. There is the spectacular dust of the demolitions carried out in the name of urban transformation—the dust that has manifested in the rubble used in creating what is now Istanbul's largest park. But then there is also the dust of this vicious demolition-construction cycle that accumulates on surfaces, which women—especially precariously employed cleaners and maids—have to deal with. Many of the cleaners and

8.
Vince Beiser, "Sand mining threatens ways of life, from Cambodia to Nigeria," *National Geographic*, April 23, 2019, https://www.nationalgeographic.com/environment/article/sand-mining-cambodia-the-lost-world-film.

9.
For an Australian example, see Adam Welz, "How ash and debris are choking Australia's rivers," *PBS News Hour*, March 3, 2020, https://www.pbs.org/newshour/science/how-ash-and-debris-are-choking-australias-rivers. For Californian examples, see Howard Hendrix, "A wildfire took my home. Trust me, California needs to stop dreaming about rising from the ashes," San Francisco Chronicle, September 5, 2021, https://www.sfchronicle.com/opinion/openforum/article/Will-California-rise-from-its-wildfire-ashes-16432682.php; Matt Wotus and Melissa Gray, "Toxic ash, debris from California wildfires pose risks during cleanup," CNN, October 29, 2017, https://edition.cnn.com/2017/10/28/us/california-wildfire-cleanup/index.html.

10.
Çaylı, "The Aesthetics of Extractivism," 1393.

maids in question come from the very working-class neighborhoods threatened with demolition.

The 2015 feature film *Toz Bezi* (Turkish for "dust cloth") engages the *particularly political* dust at work here. Its protagonists are cleaners who come from a working-class, predominantly Alevi (a constitutionally unrecognized religious minority in Turkey whose members include both Kurds and Turks) and left-leaning neighborhood located on the outskirts of the very Istanbul district of Maltepe whose coastline now hosts the gigantic new park mentioned above. The film's attention to the material particularity of dust enables a granular understanding of politics. It is the politics of gendered difference, and ultimately of the everyday as a foremost realm where dynamics otherwise deemed macropolitical (such as class and ethnicity) manifest, albeit processually and inconspicuously. This attention recalls Françoise Vergès's feminist critique of the racial Capitalocene: "In the current reworking of the geopolitics of cleanliness/dirtiness, the *invisibility* of the cleaning jobs of women of color creates the *visibility* of clean homes and public spaces."[11] *Toz Bezi* attends to how this geopolitics manifests between cleaners and their upper-middle-class women employers who perform a particular bourgeois morality by acknowledging their employee's precarity but doing little to address it. The film, itself the work of

11. Françoise Vergès, "Capitalocene, Waste, Race, and Gender," *e-flux Journal*, May 16, 2019, https://www.e-flux.com/journal/100/269165/capitalocene-waste-race-and-gender.

a women-only team, therefore invites reflection on the very gendered ethics and politics of its chosen medium, arthouse cinema. Although this form of cinema has prominently featured those at the margins of society, it has often done so by objectifying them and detaching itself from the dynamics at work in their marginalization.[12]

Visuality, then, is implicated in the questions of whether and what kind of attention is paid to dust's particular politics. When a left-leaning bookstore in the central Anatolian city of Kırşehir suffered an arson attempt in September 2015, Turkish media covered the news widely and with ample visual documentation. But it paid virtually no attention to a similar assault that took place just nine months later: unidentified assailants burning down Kurdish-language publisher Avesta's storehouse in Amed's old town, at a time when the state's counterinsurgency forces were besieging the historic city center.[13] In the summer of 2021, forest fires first devastated Marmaris, a popular tourist town on the Turkish riviera, and then, only about two weeks later, ravaged Dersim (officially: Tunceli), a predominantly Alevi city in northern Kurdistan or eastern Turkey. "Marmaris was like a film set," wrote one non-mainstream columnist, recalling all the celebrities who frequented this Mediterranean seaside town to post stories and livestream from

12. Kiraz Akın, "Aksu Bora ile Röportaj: Toz Bezi'nde Kadınlık Sınavları," 5 Harfliler, June 2, 2016, https://www.5harfliler.com/aksu-bora-ile-roportaj-toz-bezinde-kadinlik-sinavlari.

13. Tom Stevenson and Murat Bayram, "Devoted readers save the burned Kurdish books of Diyarbakır," Middle East Eye, July 19, 2016, https://www.middleeasteye.net/fr/node/54658.

the scene: "… when Dersim burns … the country sits on its butt."[14] Regions where the dust is never allowed to settle escape mainstream visualities.

An important counterpoint is the short documentary film *Şeva Xîzê* (Kurdish for "Night of the Sand"), which addresses silicosis, a long-term lung disease widespread among denim sandblasters. The disease results from long-term exposure to crystalline silica dust. In the filmmaker's words, silicosis victims "die a processual death."[15] Moreover, many also come from regions subjected to processual death on a geographical scale by violent political projects. Specifically, the silicosis victims and their relatives featured in the interviews that constitute much of *Şeva Xîzê* all come from Turkey's Kurdistan. One interviewee traces the origins of Kurdish sandblasting labor to the 1990s, when war between state forces and Kurdish guerrillas saw villages in Turkey's Kurdistan evacuated, burned down, or incorporated into the state's counterinsurgency apparatus. Villagers fled the region for metropolises, such as Istanbul, and started taking up precarious jobs, including denim manufacturing. Back home, they were exposed to the processual violence of war. The denim factories exposed them to the processual violence of racialized and precarious working conditions. *Şeva Xîzê* was filmed over a decade—in the filmmaker's words, "a ten-year-long silent process."[16]

14.
Tuğçe Tatari, "Marmaris yangınlarında ortam dizi seti gibiydi; Dersim'de yanan can can, ağaç ağaç değil mi?" T24, August 29, 2021, https://t24.com.tr/yazarlar/tugce-tatari/marmaris-yanginlarinda-ortam-dizi-seti-gibiydi-dersim-de-yanan-can-can-agac-agac-degil-mi,32273. The racialization of Turkey's Kurds was at work in the recent forest fires in more direct ways than indifference. Right-wing press and politicians blamed the forest fires in the Turkish riviera on the pro-Kurdish political movement, leading to anti-Kurdish patrols by local vigilantes. For a critical analysis of these events, see Bekir Avcı's interview with Güllistan Yarkın: "Irksallaştırılmış rejim," 1+1 Express, June 11, 2022, https://birartibir.org/irksallastirilmis-rejim/.

15.
Ezgi Sivrikaya, "Yönetmen Ali Ergül 'Kumun Gecesi'ni anlattı: Kot kumlama işçisi sağlığını istiyor!" Gazete Duvar, January 29, 2019, https://www.gazeteduvar.com.tr/sinema/2019/01/29/yonetmen-ali-ergul-kumun-gecesini-anlatti-kot-kumlama-iscisi-sagligini-istiyor.

The film interlaces interviews with footage of silicosis victims' portraits being drawn by a sand artist. Sand painting is a cultural practice central to the modern and contemporary art world's entanglement in colonial histories. Communities targeted violently by colonization, such as the Indigenous peoples of the Americas and Australasia, have long used sand painting as an embodied and nonsecular practice, but it is also one of those practices that the modern and contemporary art world has appropriated into the artistic canon, by abstracting it from the politics of sovereignty that its Indigenous use requires.[17] *Şeva Xîzê*'s use of sand painting invites associations between its subject matter and longer-standing violent histories of colonialism that implicate the canons of visual culture itself.

### Dust as Work

Dust has its own intellectual history. For at least a century now, it has captivated the imaginations of Anglophone and Francophone artists and theorists discontented with the status quo. Dust first preoccupied thinkers such as Georges Bataille and artists including Man Ray and Marcel Duchamp in the interbellum period, defined by the carnage of World War I and the Great Depression. Later, it inspired the ecological movements birthed by 1960s counterculture.[18] Today, dust seems to be undergoing

16.
Ayşegül Özbek, "'Kumun Gecesi' belgeseli erişime açıldı," Bianet, May 30, 2022, https://bianet.org/bianet/yasam/262579-kumun-gecesi-belgeseli-erisime-acildi.

17.
Khadija von Zinnenburg Carroll, *Art in the Time of Colony* (London: Routledge, 2016), 58–60.

18.
An important case in point is Agnes Denes's oeuvre associated with a period now termed "Ecovention" (a portmanteau of "ecology" and "intervention"). See Sue Spaid, *Ecovention: Current Art to Transform Ecologies* (Cincinnati, OH: The Contemporary Arts Center, 2002). Denes writes: "Dust is particulate matter, the dispersed, disordered raw material from which everything ordered and coherent arises, and it is to dust that the complex decays. From the beginning to the end, dust underlies all existence. ... Everything that we understand as consistent, the living creature, the machine, the tree, are dust in its coherent phase, part of its continuous evolutionary cycle from order to disorder, from growth to decay repeated in seemingly endless variations." See Agnes Denes, *The Human Argument: The Writings of Agnes Denes*, ed. Klaus Ottmann (Thompson, CT: Spring Publications, 2020 [2008]), 28.

a new wave of interest among intellectuals inhabiting a Global North ravaged by neoliberal austerity and confounded by climate change.[19] A thread running through this intellectual history is a commitment to dust's political potential as a critical method that problematizes modernist methodologies fixated on permanence and progress. Geographer Aya Nassar describes dust's "promise" as the troubling of "the neat division between the spectacular and the boring, the violent and the not, the eventful and the everyday. ... Dust smuggles our academic selves into modes of storytelling ... attuned to the fact the solidity of territory is a mere fantasy."[20] "I have come to see in dust a process of reconciliation," says Nassar, "dust after all is the perfect archive" ... "the excellent unraveling traveler, wearing out whatever I thought, hoped, or feared to be intact."[21] Architect Ecem Arslanay echoes this temporally focused celebration of dust: "Dust is the capturable hallmark of uncapturable time. The modern world pathologizes it. ... Dust may be deemed waste but continues to exist regardless. It is small and neglectable but, by the same token, powerful and absolute."[22] "Dust means being defeated by time. It means letting time pass without regulation ... time that accumulates in space as a layer."[23] Those who have developed and used dust as a method since the early twentieth century have therefore placed faith in its potential

19.
A useful review of this history is offered in an essay on *A Handful of Dust* (2017), an exhibition at London's Whitechapel Gallery, which wove a speculative history of the twentieth century through artworks that featured dust prominently. See Marijn Nieuwenhuis and Aya Nassar, "Dust: Perfect Circularity," Cultural Geographies, vol. 25, 3 (2018): 501–507.

20.
Aya Nassar, "A Geopoetics of Dust," Disembodied Territories, April 25, 2022, https://disembodiedterritories.com/A-Geopoetics-of-Dust.

21.
Aya Nassar, "Geopoetics as Disruptive Aesthetics: Vignettes from Cairo," GeoHumanities, vol. 7, 2 (2021): 455–463

22.
Ecem Arslanay, "Sanat ve Toz," Manifold, January 5, 2018, https://manifold.press/sanat-ve-toz.

23.
Ecem Arslanay, "Mimarlık ve Toz," Manifold, October 18, 2017, https://manifold.press/mimarlik-ve-toz.

to blur the boundaries between the temporary and the permanent or the processual and the eventful.

In a contemporary world where dust is increasingly and widely visible as a marker of the apocalypse, its capacity to fuse permanence with temporariness and eventfulness with processuality has become unquestionable. As the examples discussed above indicate, the question of dust has instead become one of a sociopolitical toll that is distributed unevenly along the axes of class, gender, and race, and which, therefore, must be understood in relation to already existing disempowerment and marginalization. It is useful to think here with historian Carolyn Steedman's book *Dust*, a critical response to Jacques Derrida's *Archive Fever*. Derrida tended to understand archive fever as a metaphorical or psychic phenomenon. Steedman invites us to reconsider it as the stuff of archival work that deals in and with dust. Understanding "archive fever" as "one that might actually be contracted in the dust of an archive" means that it is embodied and, as such, shaped by patriarchy, racism, and classism.[24] This understanding avoids the sense of a blanket carcerality and exclusion that characterizes Derrida's archive fever. It draws attention instead to how both bodies and matter are made to circulate and work and what notions of value and usefulness are assigned to them in the process. Steedman,

24. Carolyn Steedman, *Dust* (Manchester: Manchester University Press, 2001), 9. Also relevant here is Teresa Stoppani's notion of "dusting" as a political act that intervenes in state-endorsed and patriarchal orders. See Teresa Stoppani, "Antigone's Dissident Dustings: Coatings, Revolutions and the Circularity of Dust," in *Architecture and the Paradox of Dissidence*, ed. Ines Weizman (New York: Routledge, 2013), 117–127. For an earlier essay where Stoppani develops her notion of dusting, see Teresa Stoppani, "Dust revolutions: Dust, *informe*, architecture (notes for a reading of Dust in Bataille)," *The Journal of Architecture*, vol. 12, 4 (2007): 437–447.

in other words, refocuses the politics of archive-as-dust on embodied work rather than on dust's physical properties or critical interpretation alone.

I wish to extend this refocusing to the constituencies that have figured in this essay: the sandblasting workers forced to inhale the dust that kills them gradually; the unpaid domestic workers burdened with the dust of sand quarries; the precariously employed cleaners and maids expected to collect the dust of urban transformation both in the working-class neighborhoods targeted by the construction sector and in the upper-middle-class ones where they work; various inhabitants of racialized geographies that violent political projects seek to reduce to dust. The histories of violence that have imbricated race, class, and patriarchy with one another continue to wreak planetary-ecological havoc to the disproportionate detriment of marginalized communities and burden them with the task of cleaning up, recovering from, and giving meaning to the detritus. Dust materializes a contradiction fundamental to this violent imbrication's current iteration. Dust is what only dustwork can deal with—collective, embodied work that is both unrecognized by the violent forces that produce the dust in the first place and essential to their sustenance.

*Dr. Eray Çaylı is Professor of Human Geography with a Focus on Violence and Security in the Anthropocene at the University of Hamburg.*

Black Ink
This black ink was prepared by mixing one part gum arabic to two parts distilled water until a thick, viscous solution was formed. Then black ash taken from a book burned on June 10, 2016 in an attack on a Kurdish publishing house in the city of Diyarbakır was added. The ash was steadily mixed into the solution over a period of several hours to create a paste of uniform consistency. A further measure of distilled water was added and the mixture left to blend for four days with regular stirring until a fine, glossy ink was achieved.
A measure of soot from a razed house was added to the book ash to deepen the colour.

p. 63, 65–67:

***Black Ink***, 2019
Typographic print made with ink created from burned book ashes
31.5 × 20.5 cm

## Black Ink

This black ink was prepared by mixing one part gum arabic to two parts distilled water until a thick, viscous solution was formed. Then black ash taken from a book burned on June 10, 2016 in an attack on a Kurdish publishing house in the city of Diyarbakır was added. The ash was steadily mixed into the solution over a period of several hours to create a paste of uniform consistency. A further measure of distilled water was added and the mixture left to blend for four days with regular stirring until a fine, glossy ink was achieved.

A measure of soot from a razed house was added to the book ash to deepen the colour.

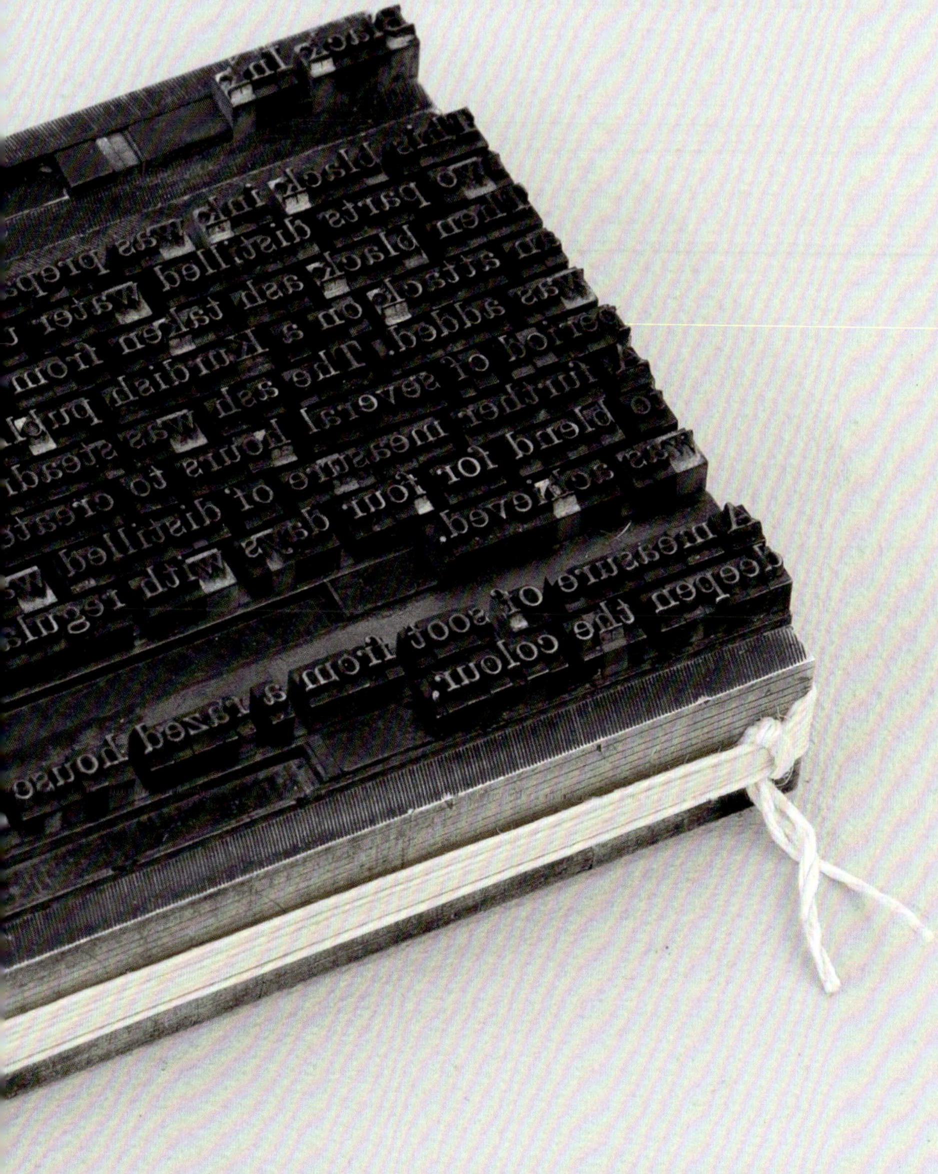

# On Falling Quickly

HEATHER DAVIS

> ...
> and our land, in its bloodied night,
> is a jewel that glimmers for the far upon the far
> and illuminates what's outside it ...
> —MAHMOUD DARWISH, "To Our Land"

Normally, dust does not fall quickly. It tends to hover in the air, catching the light, moving, and drifting on various currents. It comes to settle, slowly and relentlessly. Dust is often made of a mixture of dead skin cells, dust mites, dead insect particles, soil, pollen, microplastics, bacteria, hair, and clothing fibers. The dust referenced in Fatma Bucak's *While the Dust Quickly Falls* is much more specific. This is a dust that falls at a different rate with a different intensity. It is the dust that appears after a bombing, the dust from the deliberate burning associated with conflict, the dust of ravaging wildfires, the dust, almost impossible to brush off and insistently accumulating, of how these atrocities feed into and exacerbate each other. This dust is falling quickly, weighted.

The dust has accumulated, in the largest gallery of the exhibition, into a mountain. Sourced from the Kurdish-majority province Tunceli, the installation is a mixture of ash and soil. It speaks to the innumerable acts of violence and neglect that have gone into its composition: the legacies of wildfires in 2021 exacerbated by climate change and the intense and brutal conflict between the Turkish army and the Kurdistan Workers' Party (PKK) in the 1990s. The war's effects had already damaged the land even before it burned. Both events reverberated through the soil, depleting it, and eating away at biodiversity. In *The Three Ecologies*, Félix Guattari speaks of the intertwining of environmental, psychic, and social well-being, bringing an ecological perspective of diversity to all three realms as a measure of health.[1] Throughout the exhibition, there is a deep attention to how these three ecologies inform each other, how the psychic and the social influence the Earth, and vice versa. This is particularly emphasized through the deep feeling of ancestral connection to land, the interrelatedness of cultures that are both human and other-than-human, and the various catastrophes that have interrupted those relations. In other words, what happens to the land, plants, and soil reverberates within human communities. Our bodies emerge from and with the air, the water, and the land, and return to them. We cannot separate ourselves. Yet, the dust accumulates and begins to suffocate.

A two-channel video, *They burned it all*, plays on a loop, with each channel mutually informing

1. Félix Guattari, *The Three Ecologies* (London: Continuum, 2008).

the other. The title, *They burned it all*, references the intense fires that ripped through the region while also alluding to how fire is used in war. While fire is an ordinary and even necessary part of the ecosystem, allowing for regrowth and regeneration, if fires burn too hot, they can contribute to soil erosion or, at worst, kill off the necessary bacteria and mycelium that keep the soils alive. These recent fires have been coming too hot and too quickly. The massive fires in 2017, 2021, and 2022 have led the European Union's scientists to declare the Mediterranean a "wildfire hotspot."[2]

In *They burned it all*, Bucak crawls across the ashes of what was once a forest floor, closely examining the remnants. The color palette of the former forest has been reduced to grey, black, cream, and some remaining reds from leaves in the background. There is nothing green here. Trees appear broken. Bucak leans in close, carefully digging a small hole to look at what might still be there, just beneath this dust. She puts her ear to the ground, listening for what might not be seen, and the video is interrupted by a close-up shot of a singer's mouth and throat as she attempts to clear her throat. It seems as if she is about to speak or sing, but instead, the video cuts back to Bucak crawling on the ground. She continues the journey painstakingly and slowly, looking for a place to listen to the earth. Again, the scene cuts to the mouth and throat of someone who

2. Kate Abnett, "Mediterranean has become a 'wildfire hotspot', EU scientists say," Reuters, August 4, 2021, https://www.reuters.com/business/environment/mediterranean-has-become-wildfire-hotspot-eu-scientists-say-2021-08-04/.

looks like they are trying to emit a noise but are unable to. The mouth opens and closes, like a fish out of water. The land, the soil, is unable to speak or to be heard, even by attentive, painstaking, active listening, and this muteness has been transmitted to the person depicted. Something has been cut.

The other channel begins with a voice saying "totally silent" ... "It was very difficult, you know, to be silent" as the video shows a black stage, curtain, and music stands. A group of ten performers enter the stage, approach the stands, clear their throats, chat, and adjust the microphones. After announcing that they are ready, they stand still, in pairs, behind the stands and microphones, looking into the camera, mouths stubbornly closed, and remain silent. We hear the extra-diegetic sounds of a vocal performance overlaid on the image to eerie effect. The song is the Kurdish translation of the phrase "they burned it all" sung letter by letter. The painstaking enunciation of the sentence speaks to the ongoing violence and repression in the region, and the use of fire as a weapon of erasure. It also evokes the beauty of language and culture as a tool of resistance. It shows the gaps between silence and speech, where music intercedes.

So much of this work is about what cannot be said, cannot be spoken. It is either out of sync, or too slow, or the voice is gone. Compositional scores feature prominently in several of the artworks. Still, the voice, the ability to put things into a recognizable language that might take place in a public sphere, is absent. The artworks speak to the relationship between presence and absence, what can or cannot be said, what is trying to be said, but there are no words, no sounds that can be made that are adequate, that can capture the intensity of feeling, the immense loss. In the moments when vocalization is possible, it is displaced and unembodied. The ongoing removal from the land, and the processes of desertification through climate change and war, reflect a resounding silence entering the world, the silence of the massive loss of species, the silence that comes in the wake of the ripping and tearing of a fire out of control, the silence of lost or repressed cultural knowledge and practice. But song and musicality also intrude into this silence, even if it carries an elegiac quality.

In Catriona Mortimer-Sandilands's essay "Queer Melancholia," she describes the process of having to figure out ways to "grieve the ungrievable." Many people have largely been abandoned, including refugees and disenfranchised people in the Mediterranean basin, where the deaths are not mourned but are considered a normal state of affairs. Similarly, there are very few practices of mourning the lives of other-than-humans within a modernist framework as they occupy a position outside the realms of care or protection. Both the other-than-human world and oppressed peoples are "ungrievable." It is, therefore, important, Mortimer-Sandilands argues, to keep open the process of mourning as a political act of refusal. Melancholy, which according to Freud is one stage in a cycle of grief that moves towards letting go, betterment, and progress, is transformed in Mortimer-Sandilands's work—and the work of the AIDS activists that she draws upon—to articulate how not "getting over" and instead choosing to keep the mourning alive is a political act that can be transformative in a larger sense. She writes, "Melancholia is not only a denial of the loss of a beloved object but also a potentially politicized way of preserving that object in the midst of a culture that fails to recognize its significance."[3] There is a similar ethic in Bucak's performances, creating rituals for the ungrievable other-than-human world, unresolved, on display as an open wound and a possibility for things to be otherwise.

Bucak also constantly reminds us of the interconnections between the human and other-than-human worlds. There is a common plant in many parts of the world colloquially called fireweed. It appears after fires, but also after bombs. While not included in the exhibition, fireweed seems to flutter in the background of this exhibition,

3. Catriona Mortimer-Sandilands, "Melancholy Natures, Queer Ecologies," in *Queer Ecologies: Sex, Nature, Politics, Desire*, ed. Catriona Mortimer-Sandilands and Bruce Erickson (Bloomington, IN: Indiana University Press, 2010), 333.

thriving in the disturbed soil. Numerous other plants also appear under conditions of extreme stress, endangerment, or extinction. For example, *Damascus rose* (2016–ongoing), is a project that attempts to cultivate roses from Syria. These flowers were once beloved but had been largely abandoned during the ongoing civil war. Bucak took over a hundred cuttings and grafted them onto European plants as strange new hybrids attempting to survive in foreign conditions. This act brings attention to the fact that it is not only "wild" species that are threatened in the ongoing catastrophe of the sixth great extinction event, but also domestic species. The events that bring about species collapse are not neutral, but intimately tied to ongoing histories of colonialism, capitalism, and war. *Damascus rose* highlights to the interrelations between cultural attachments and whether or not a particular plant thrives. Plants have long been metaphors for human movement, through designations of native or invasive, often with racist or xenophobic overtones. Here, the hybrid roses offer a new way of looking at these questions. The roses and refugees are both deracinated, without roots to push into the earth, living in grafted conditions, struggling to survive and adapt. The hybrid plant offers a multi-located perspective that can be useful but also requires more care and more resources from gallery attendants.

There are many underlying reasons for human migration and the precarity of these roses including war and climate change. Syria is a prime example of climate change's impact on pre-existing issues such as political instability, poverty, and scarce resources. Previously home to lush agricultural land, Syria has had three major droughts since the 1980s. The most recent stretched from 2006 to 2010 and was recorded as the worst multi-year drought in 900 years. This led to widespread food shortages, exacerbating previously existing tensions and inequalities, contributing to the conflict and massive migration. Climate change is increasingly an underlying cause of war, while the changing landscape only worsens dire or difficult conditions for those displaced by war.

Powerful and beautiful, Bucak's work makes the connections between war and climate change, people and other-than-humans, poignantly felt. It draws heavily on a politicized melancholia that is, in fact, a preservation of life "whose ghost propels a changed understanding of the present."[4] It does not shy away from the potential horrors of that transformation but also refuses to give in.

4. Ibid.

*Dr. Heather Davis is an Assistant Professor of Culture and Media at Eugene Lang College, The New School.*

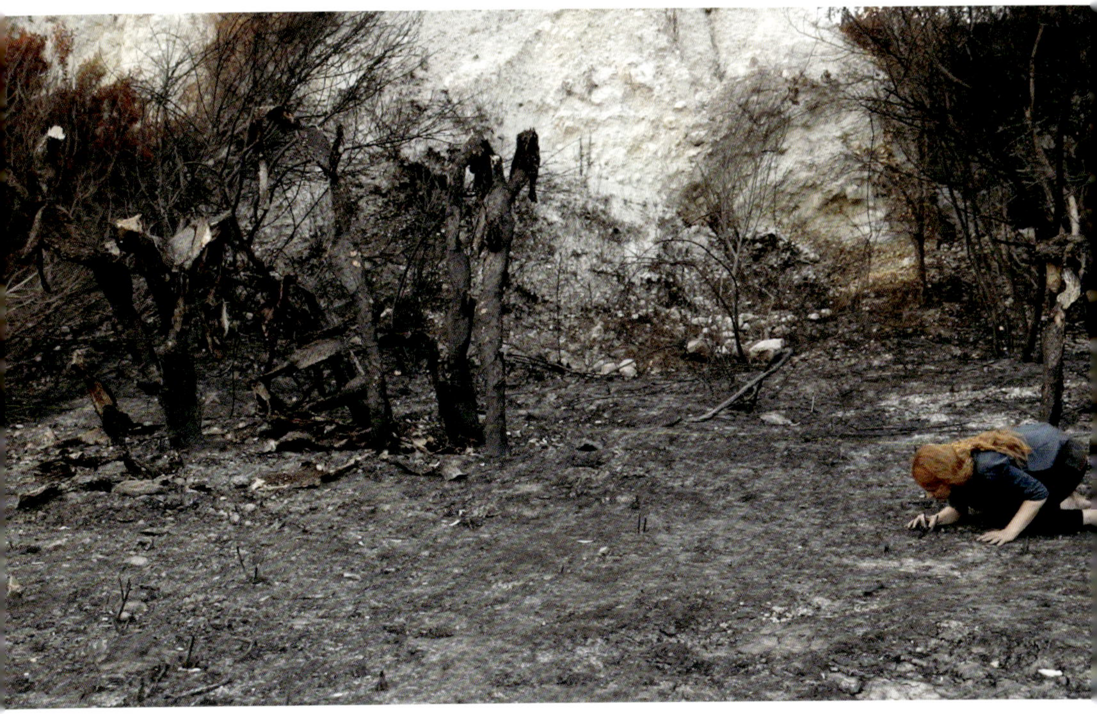

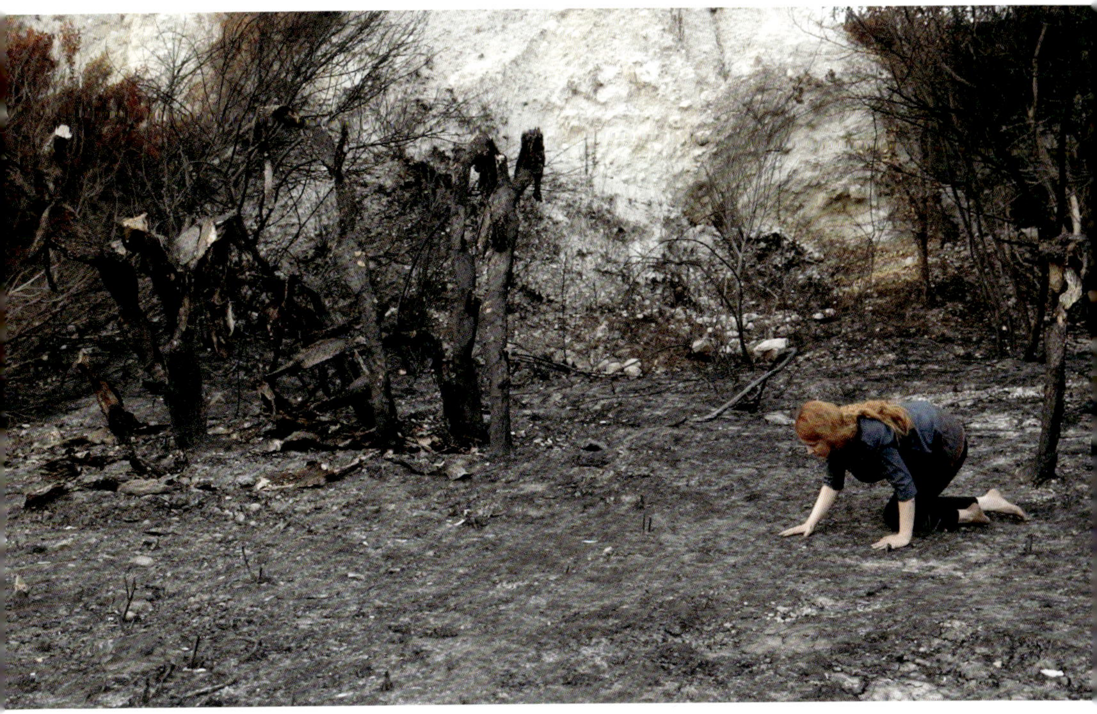

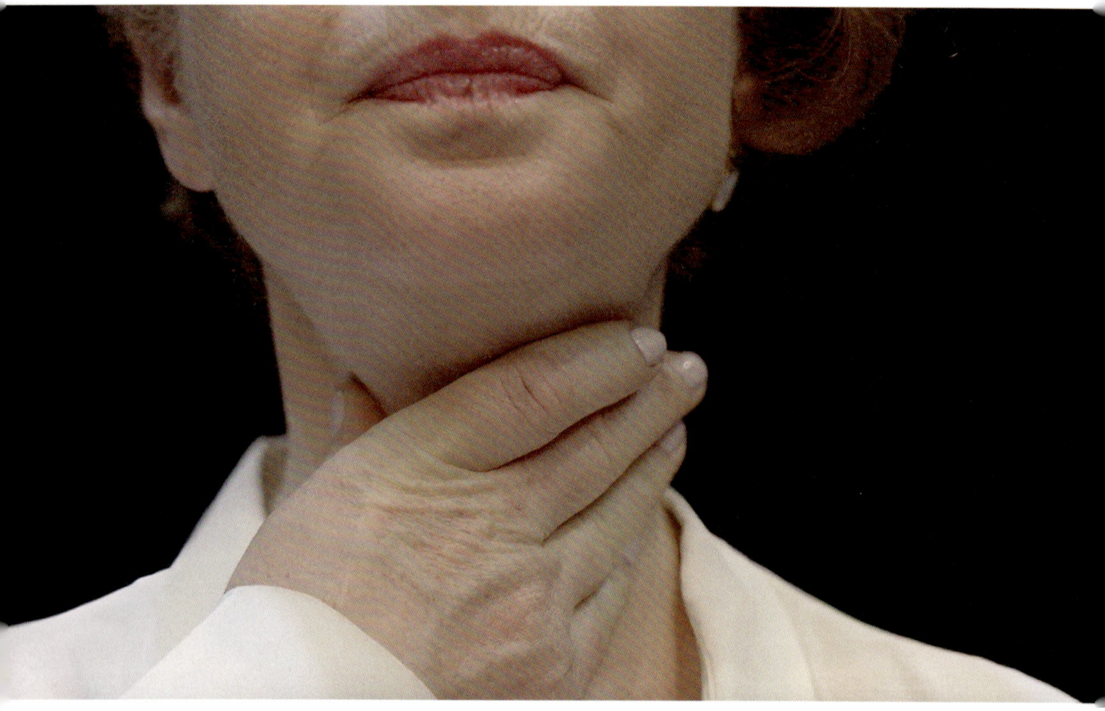

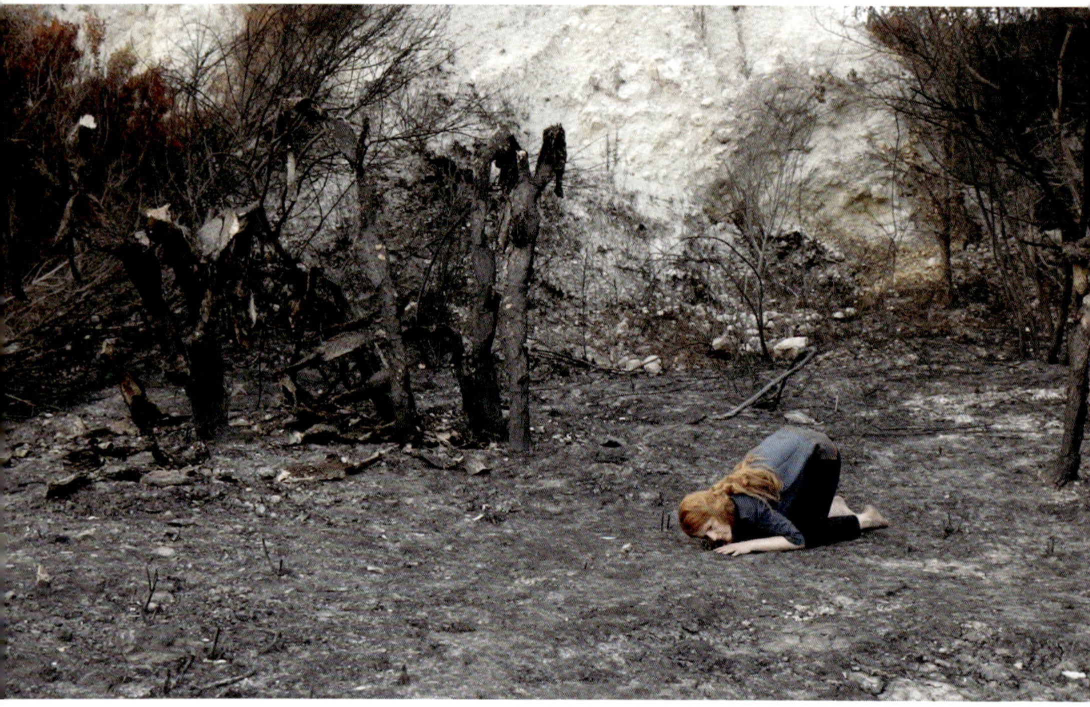

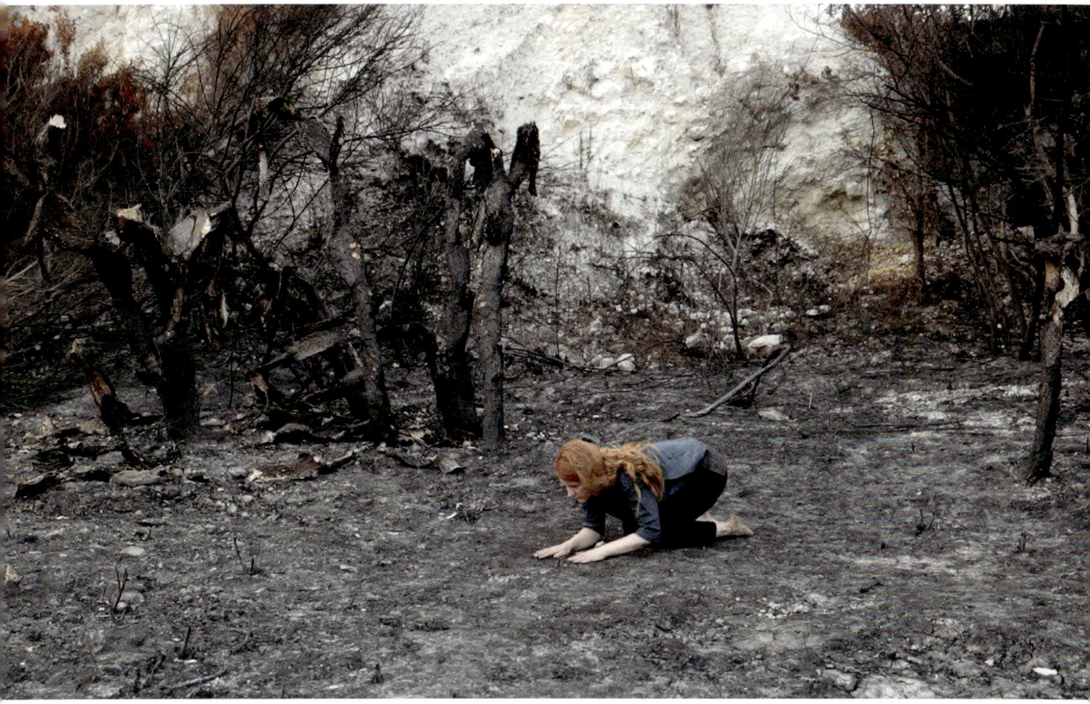

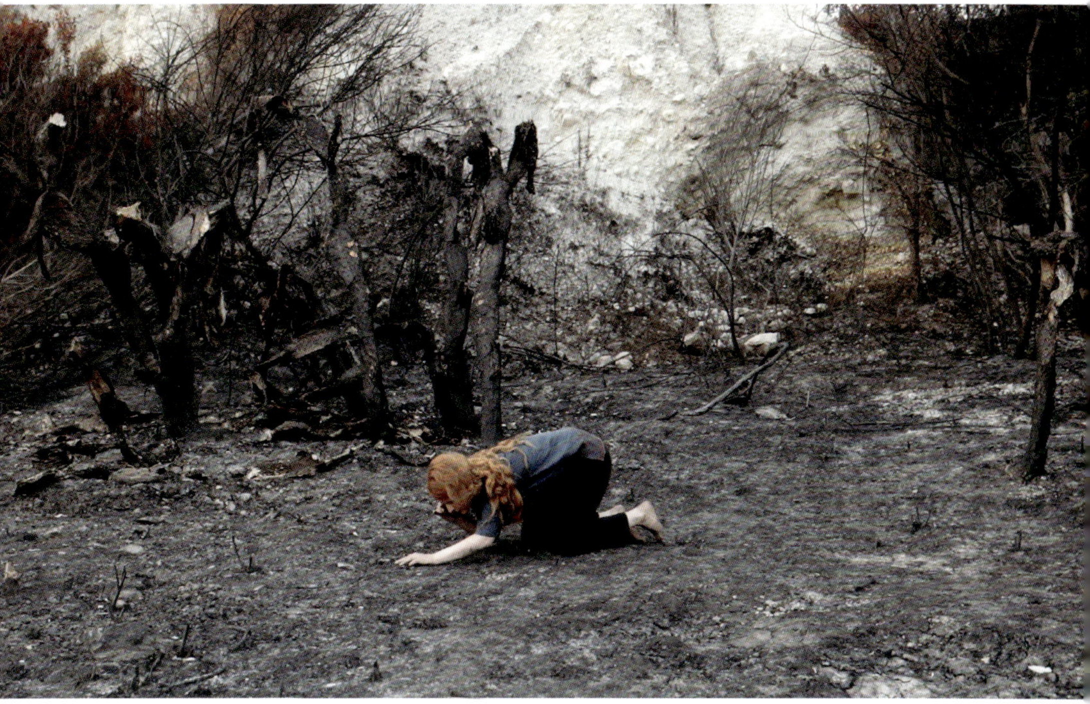

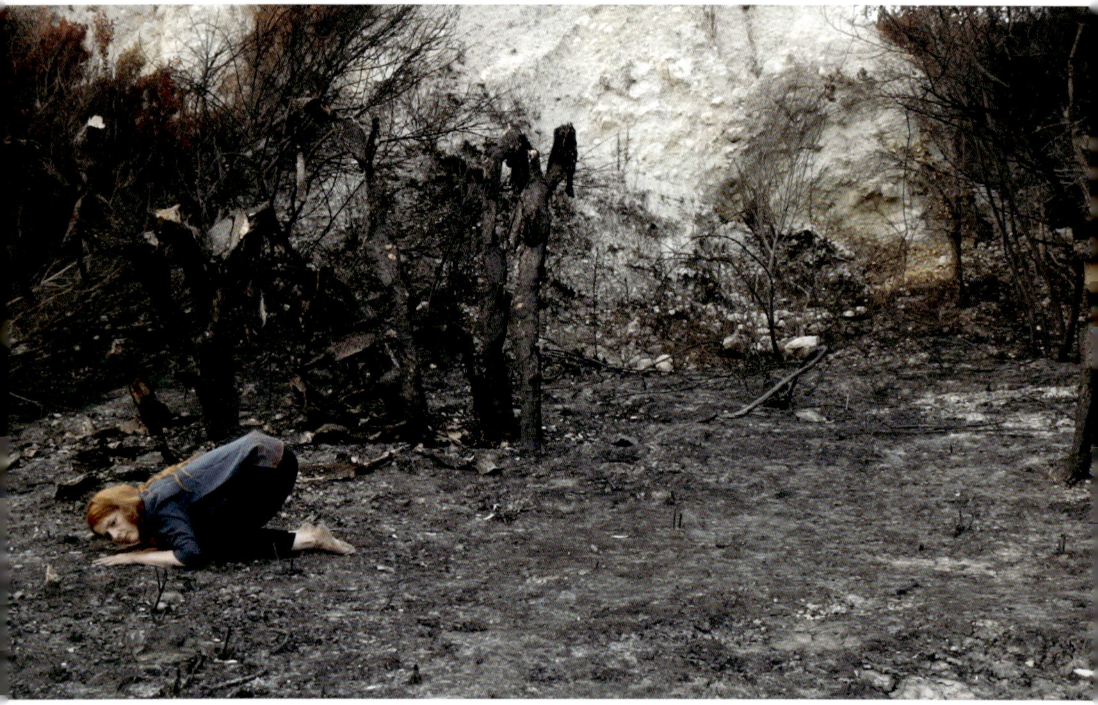

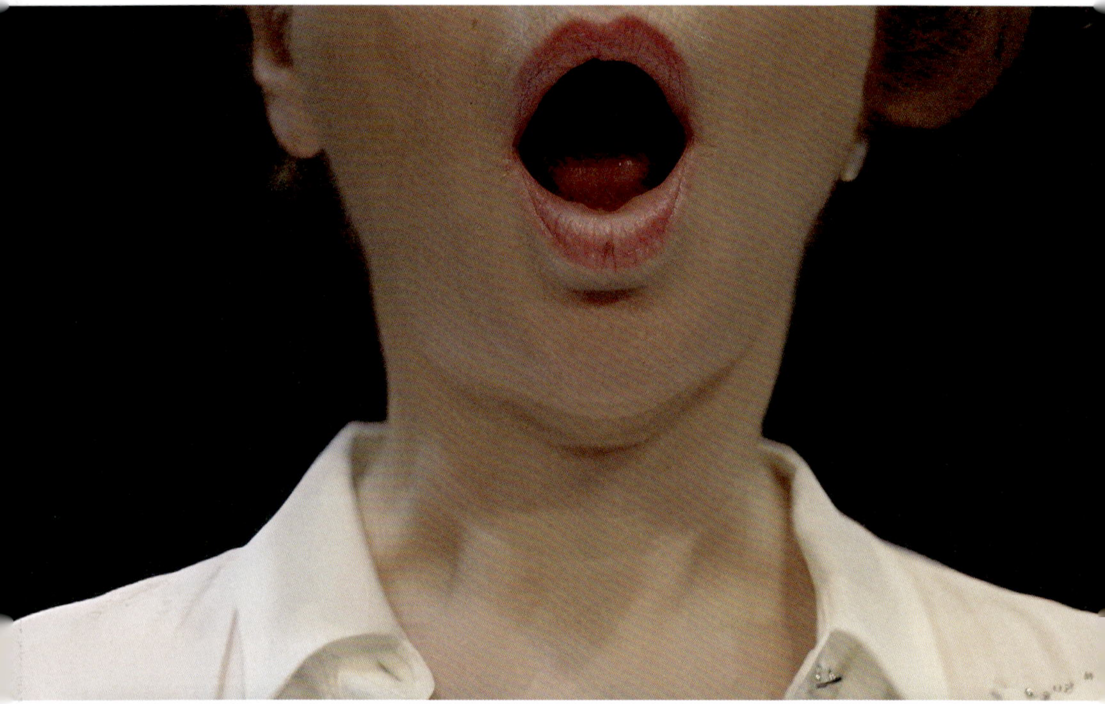

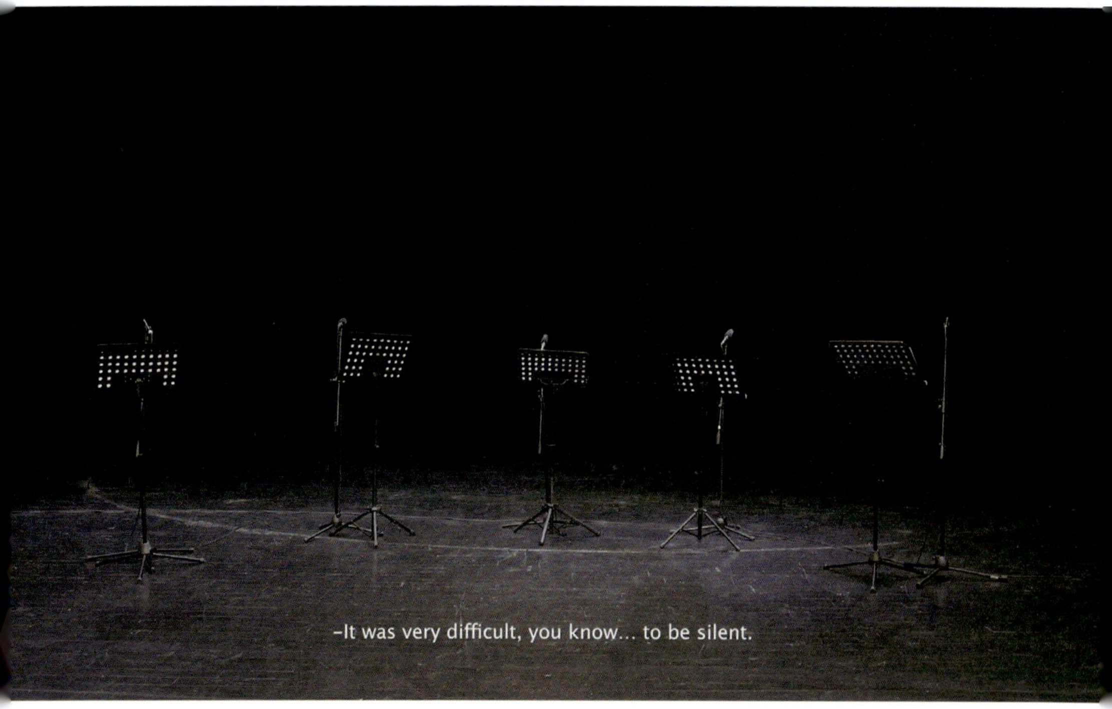
–It was very difficult, you know… to be silent.

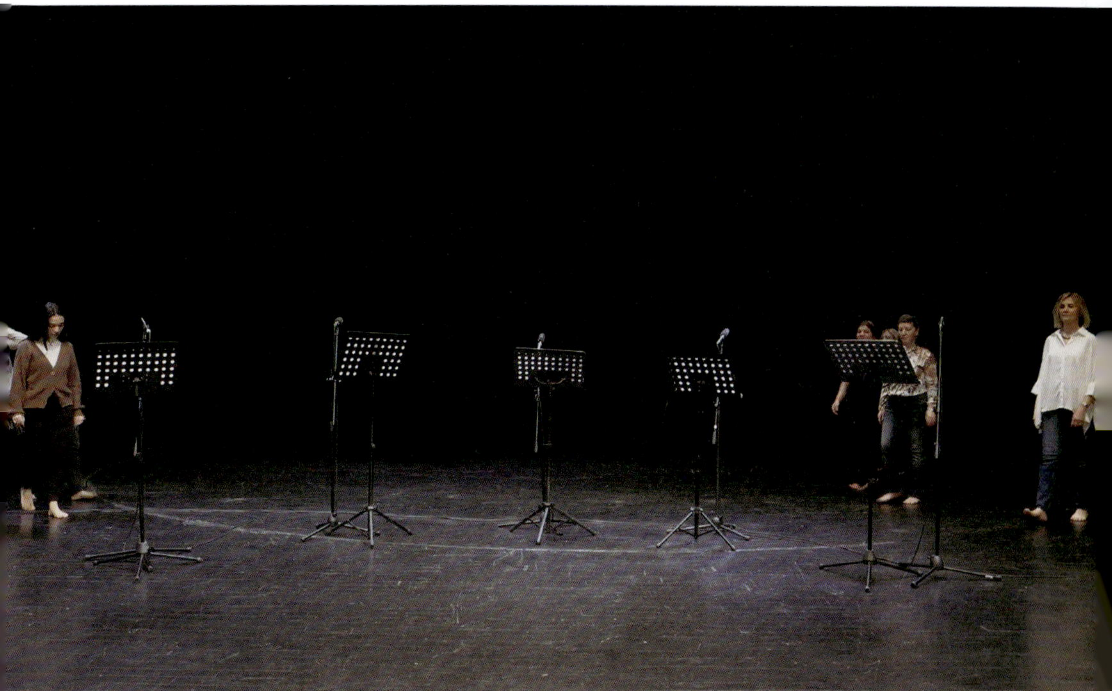

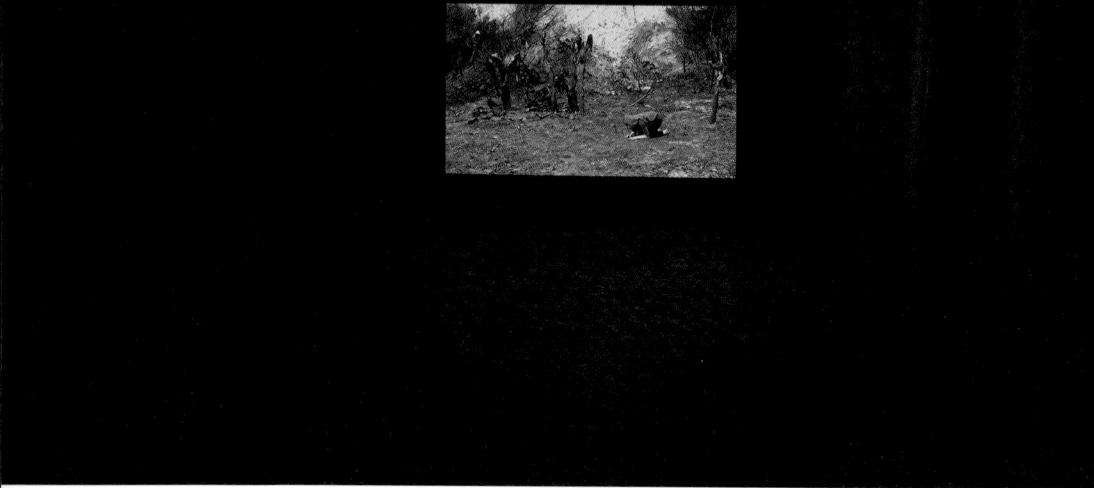

p. 77–85:

***They burned it all***, 2022
Two-channel video installation
4' 17" and 8' 47"
Project realized with the support of the Italian Council (2022)

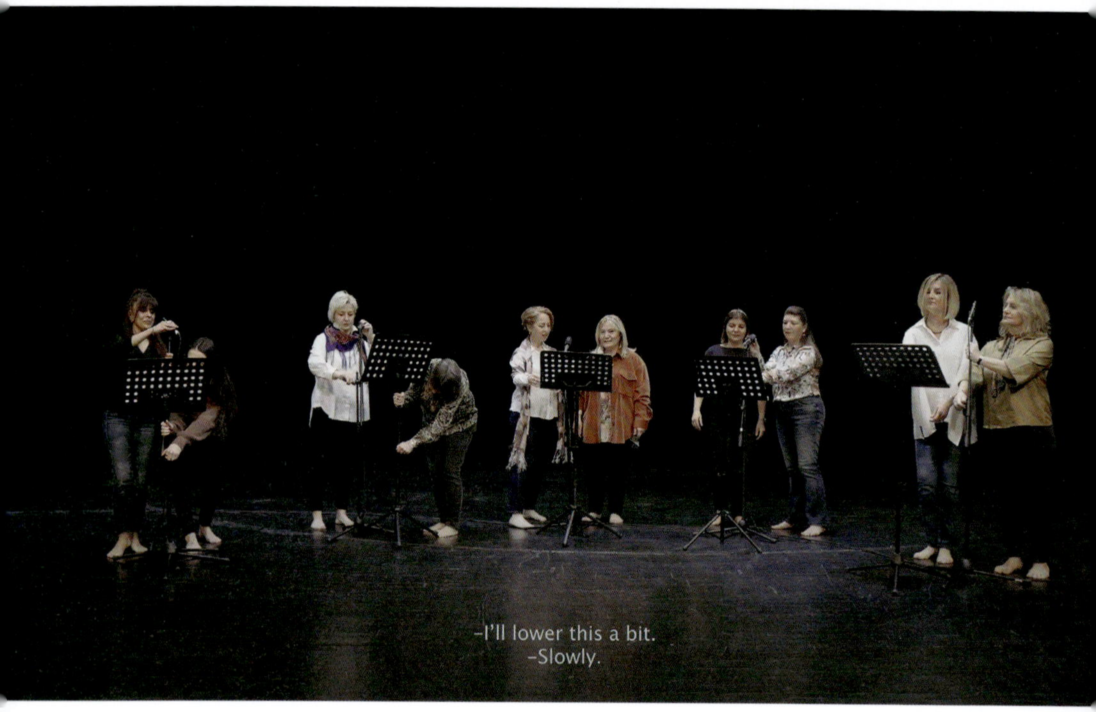
-I'll lower this a bit.
-Slowly.

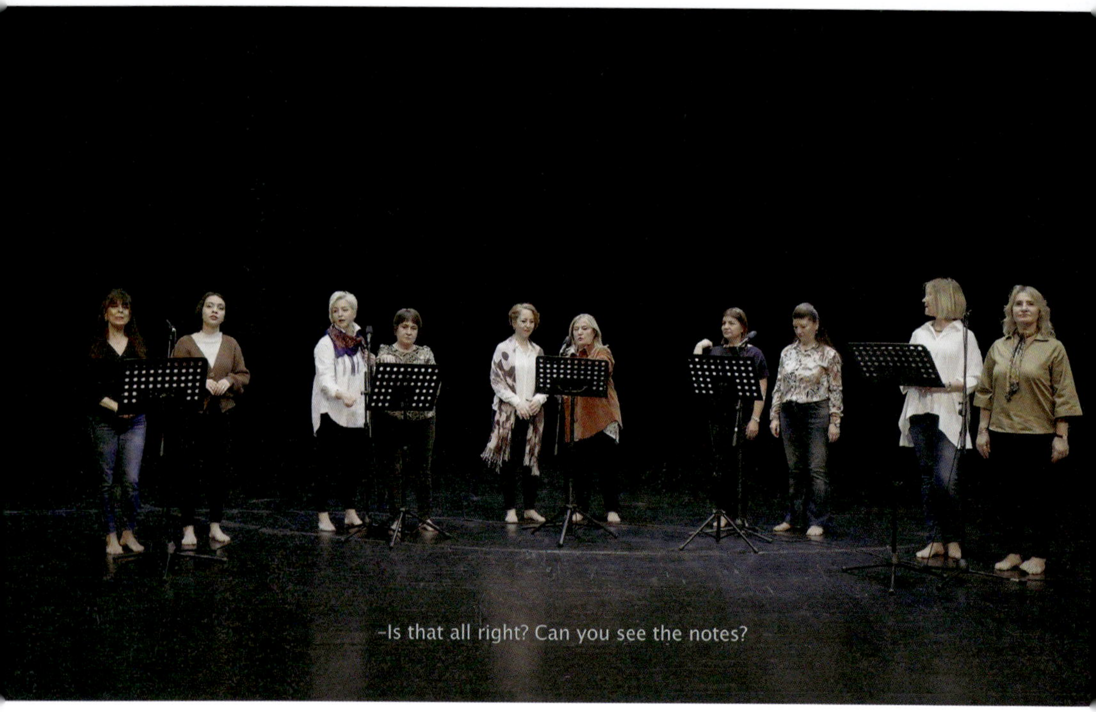
-Is that all right? Can you see the notes?

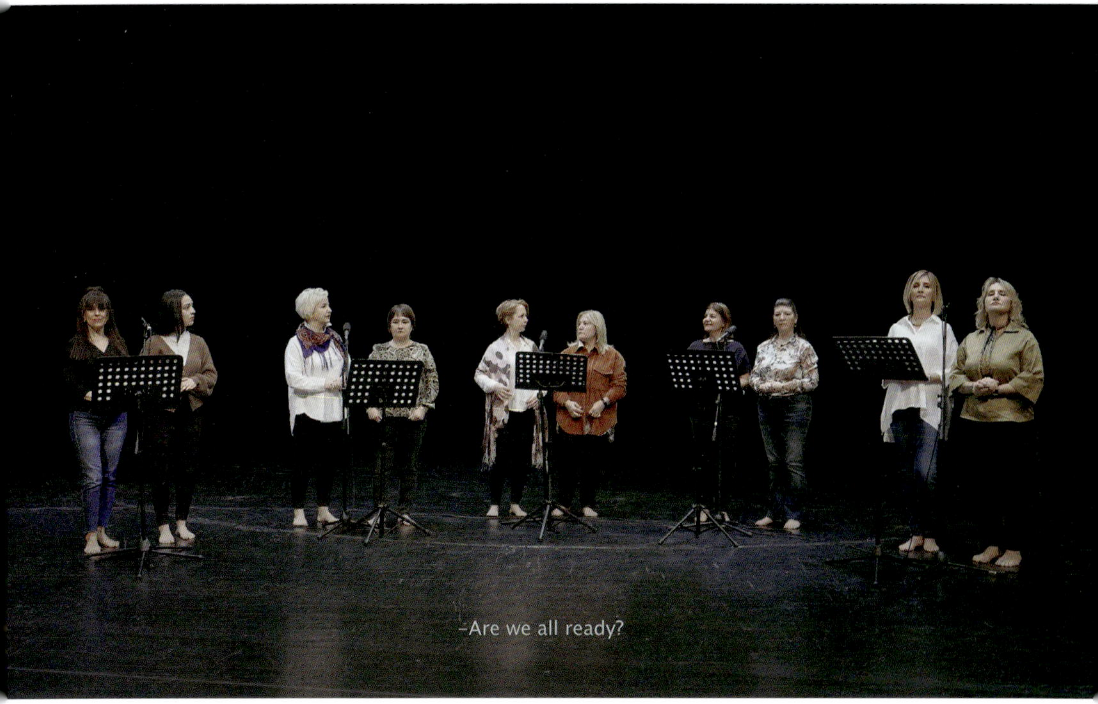
–Are we all ready?

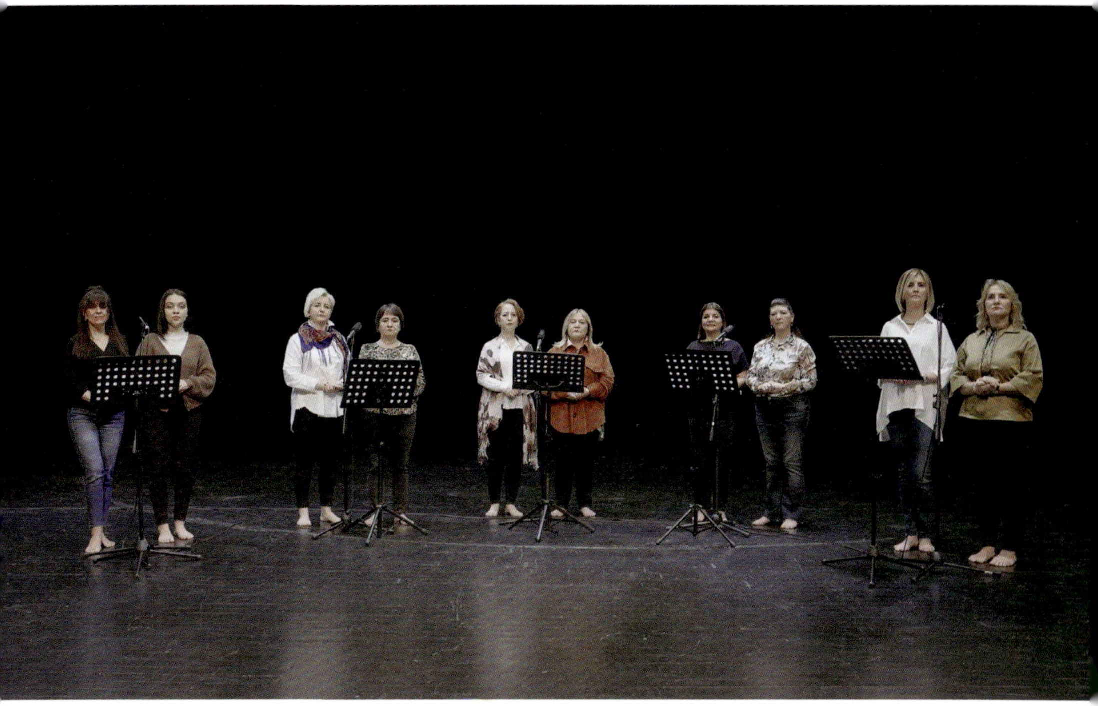

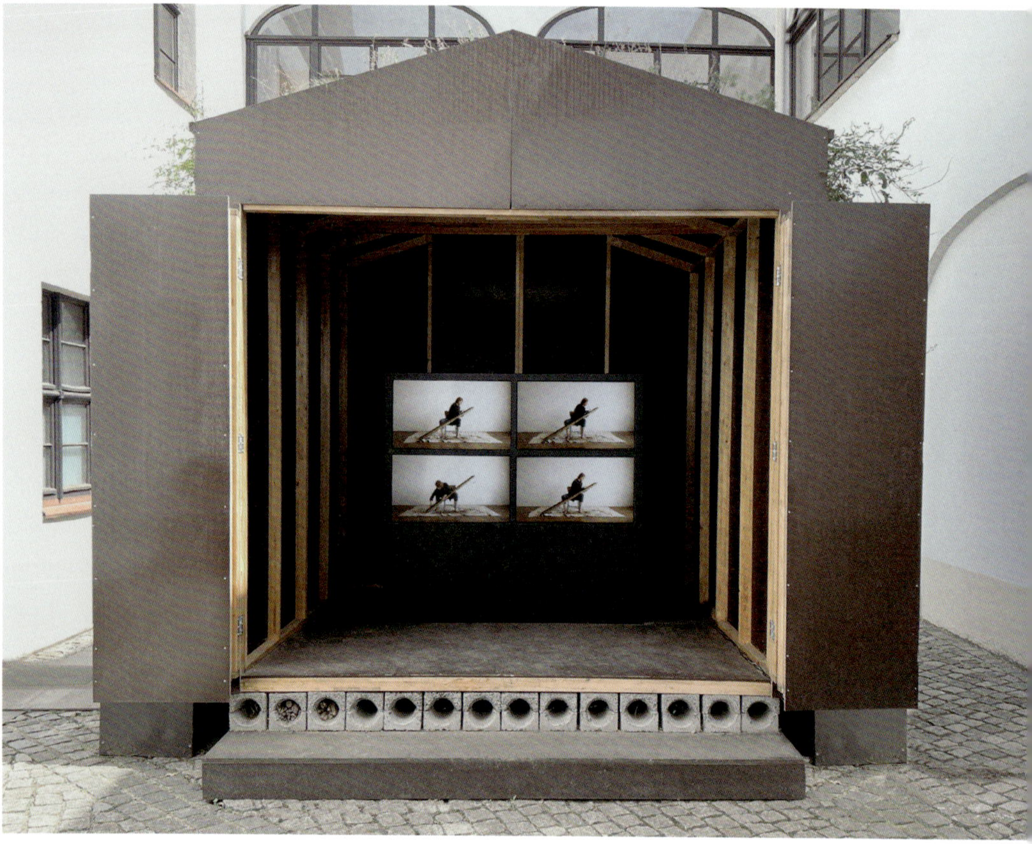

p. 86, 91–93:

***Hate to disturb this precious silence***, 2021
Four-channel video installation
10' 31", 13' 16", 13' 21", and 8' 14"

# Capitalocene in Prestissimo

ECEM ARSLANAY

> If we'd expended as much energy trying to find out how to communicate with trees as we have devoted to the extraction and transformation of petroleum, perhaps we'd be capable of lighting up a city by photosynthesis, or feeling vegetal sap run in our veins, but our Western civilization has specialized in capital and domination, in carbon energy and extractivism, in taxonomy and identification, not in cooperation or transformation.
> —PAUL B. PRECIADO*

Fatma Bucak "makes a plank talk" in her video installation *Hate to disturb this precious silence*. Her sanding gives voice to a wooden board, which once was a part of a tree—a tree with millionfold nodes of growth, daily-clock genes, and expanding rings of timekeeping. It had experience pollinating insects, microbes, fungi, herbivores, and other plants; as well as communication methods that use volatile organic compounds, electrical signaling, chemical cues, and mycorrhizal networks.

What turns an animate subject (a tree) into an inanimate object (wood board)? Physically, it is sawing. Cognitively, it is taxonomy-oriented thinking and a conceptual operation of sawing. It is an act of exclusion, of othering, of positing a hierarchical system of being. Bucak puts forward the complex ontology of a common artifact. She activates a muted,

* From a talk at Glad Day Bookshop, Toronto, January 22, 2020, launching *An Apartment on Uranus*

objectified, exploited part of a tree. It speaks in waves of aural textures, a language ungraspable to the human intellect. But its manifold moods can be deciphered, for they speak directly to the human psyche—a vast, vigorous enigma that can only be partially known, inaptly rationalized, and irrationally disciplined.

It is a haptic contact that extricates the esoteric knowledge of the plank. In Bucak's soothing hands, the sander she uses is a ritualistic gizmo, a healing apparatus, and a shamanic means. In a way, she decolonizes this tool, which was meant to smooth, discipline, and impose standard forms, forcing things into solid meanings so they can be efficiently grasped and subjugated. A state of generous listening is more apparent in the video *They burned it all*, in which an on-stage chorus faces the artist, who is crawling on a charred Mediterranean forest floor. She scans the earth with her hands and ears, looking for revelations that do not come. From the other channel, we hear a melodic clamor. Its source remains unknown, for the chorus is silent.

Humans have long spoken in place of what they labeled as "nature." With his symphonies for strings, Antonio Vivaldi tried to sound like spring's singing birds and serene streams, summer's suffocating heat and abrupt storms, autumn's harvest festivity, and winter's icy winds. In his Pastoral Symphony, Ludwig van Beethoven imitated the sensations of rural landscapes, while Richard Strauss described climbing a mountain in his Alpine Symphony. All with human-centered storytelling.

In Bucak's immersive installation *Numbing silence covers us like fine dust*, the soil itself is heard, with all its residents, living or dead, inextricably entangled. It is multispecies storytelling. The traumatized earth taken from Tunceli, a devastated conflict-scape, can also be smelled and seen. These are delicate scents—glimpses of oppressive stories. In the installation, burned-out soil speaks. Instead of the on-stage microphones in *They burned it all*, this time buried microphones are at play. They capture the deserted noises of the underworld, rendering it a stage. The minimal ambient track is the charging, discharging, barreling, colliding, and accelerating sounds of the Capitalocene. It is a subatomic noise. A stellar noise. A cosmological noise reverberating through the vast site of human agency. A slow, husky tone of speedy resonance, it is spurred by the restless petro-capitalist engine. An engine that makes plastics from prehistoric, petrified bodies. An engine that makes fresh toxic flesh from plastics. An engine whose exploitative pursuit of profit is based on war and invasion, death and decay. Death is the perpetual rearrangement of atoms, for matter has a circular economy. But the engine adds new radioactive isotopes to this prudent math. It then expedites them all, troubling all the living and the non-living down to their nuclei, making time atomic.

The zeptosecond, today's smallest unit of time, is a trillionth of a billionth of a second, the rate at which a photon moves through a hydrogen molecule. All clocks are based on an oscillator, a frequency that ticks regularly, something that always returns to the starting point in the same amount of time. This can also be said of a group of flowers. Swedish botanist Carl Linnaeus, who separated plants according to their opening and closing times, had such a project. All perceived frequencies of nature have organized the small clocks of humankind through the ages, for humanity was no separate entity. Now, it is. For the flow of production, the petro-capitalist engine has recalibrated human clocks with great precision, unit by unit on a global scale, so ambitiously that it managed to affect a much larger operation than itself. With its tiny, greedy clocks, it has forced the earth's geological clock to speed up. It changed the climate and created its own extinction. It built a time bomb, a Doomsday Clock.

*While the Dust Quickly Falls* is not entirely about this apocalyptic panorama; it is about the "ecosystem-destroying, human and animal labor-transforming, multispecies soul-mutilating, epidemic-friendly, corn-monocrop-promoting, cross-species heartbreaking"[1] systems. But when dealing with earth's troubled skin and everything that grows on it, it focuses on the rich ground for contact, reconciliation, and multispecies healing.

1. Donna Jeanne Haraway, *Staying with the Trouble: Making Kin in the Chthulucene* (Durham, NC: Duke University Press, 2016).

*Ecem Arslanay is a writer and editor based in Istanbul.*

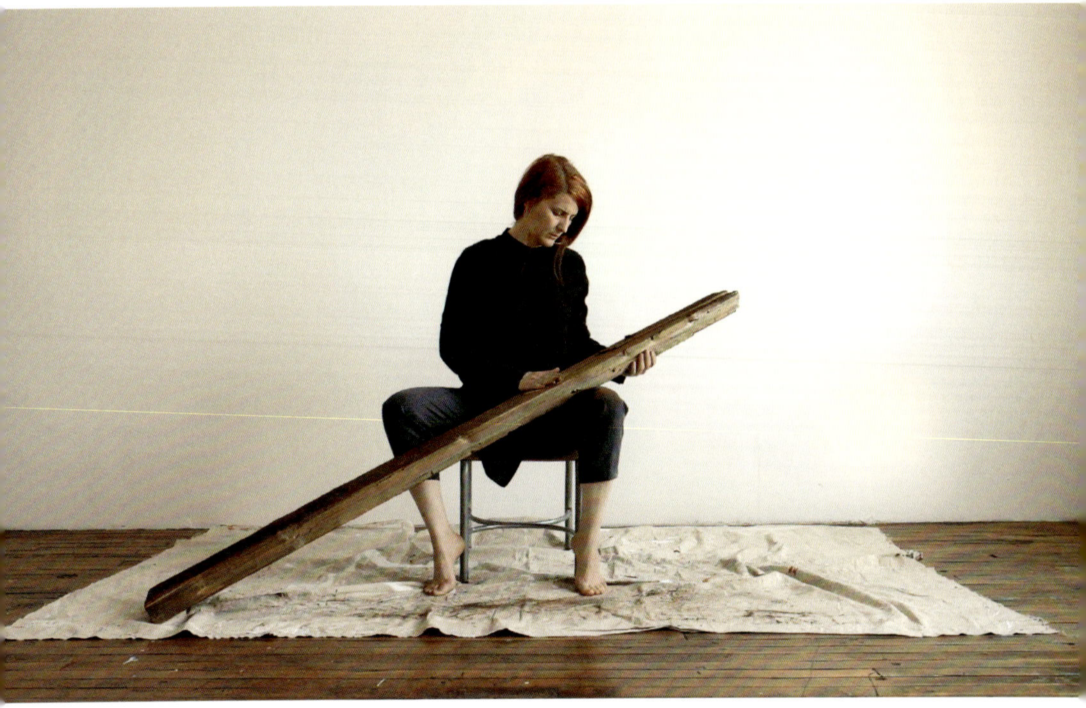

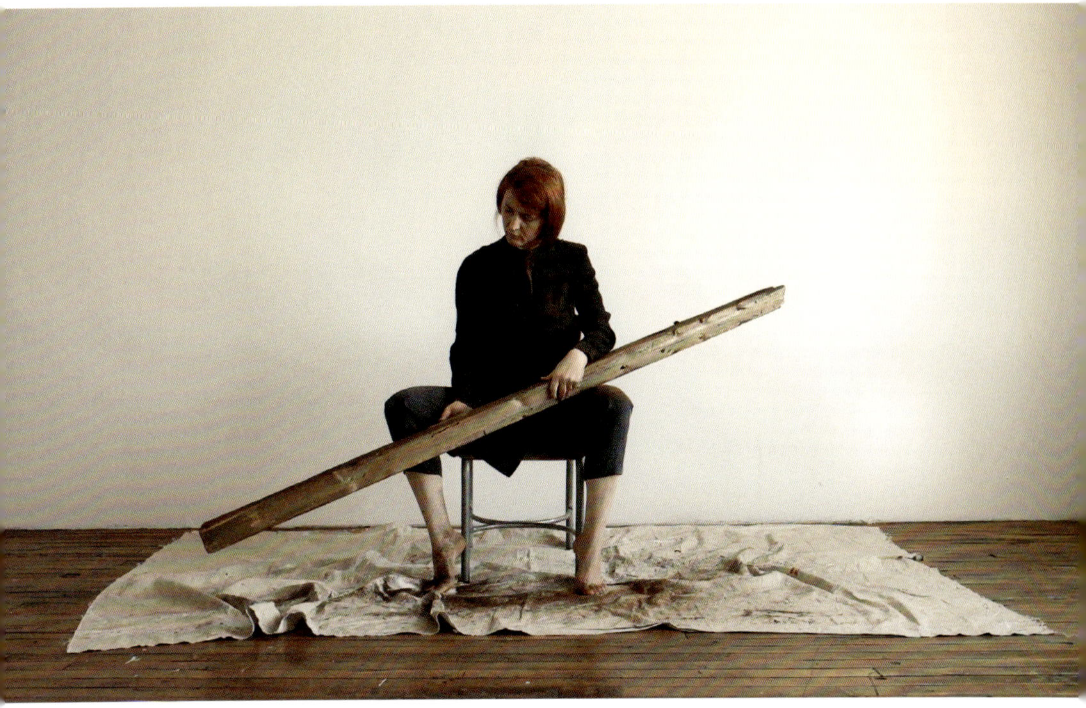

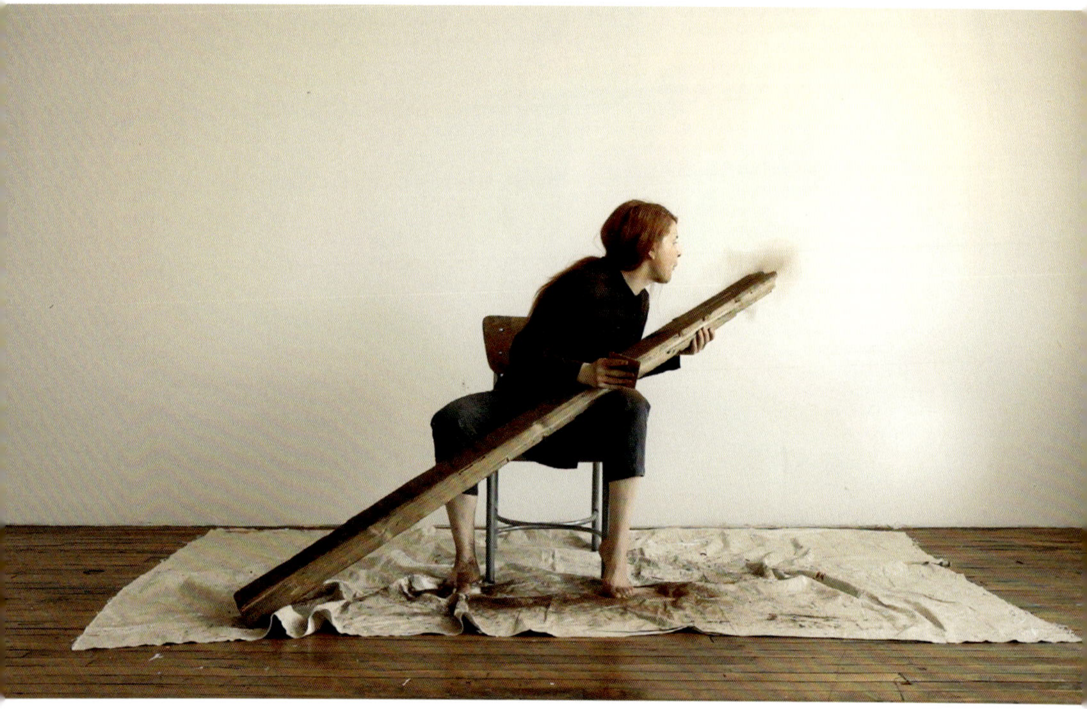

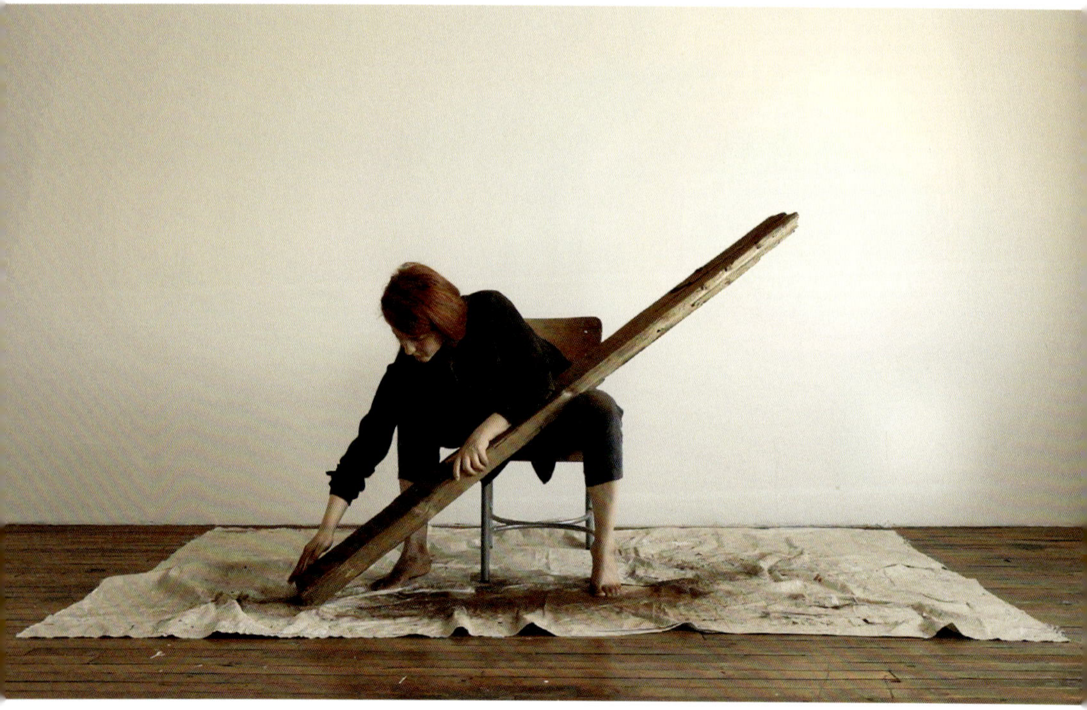

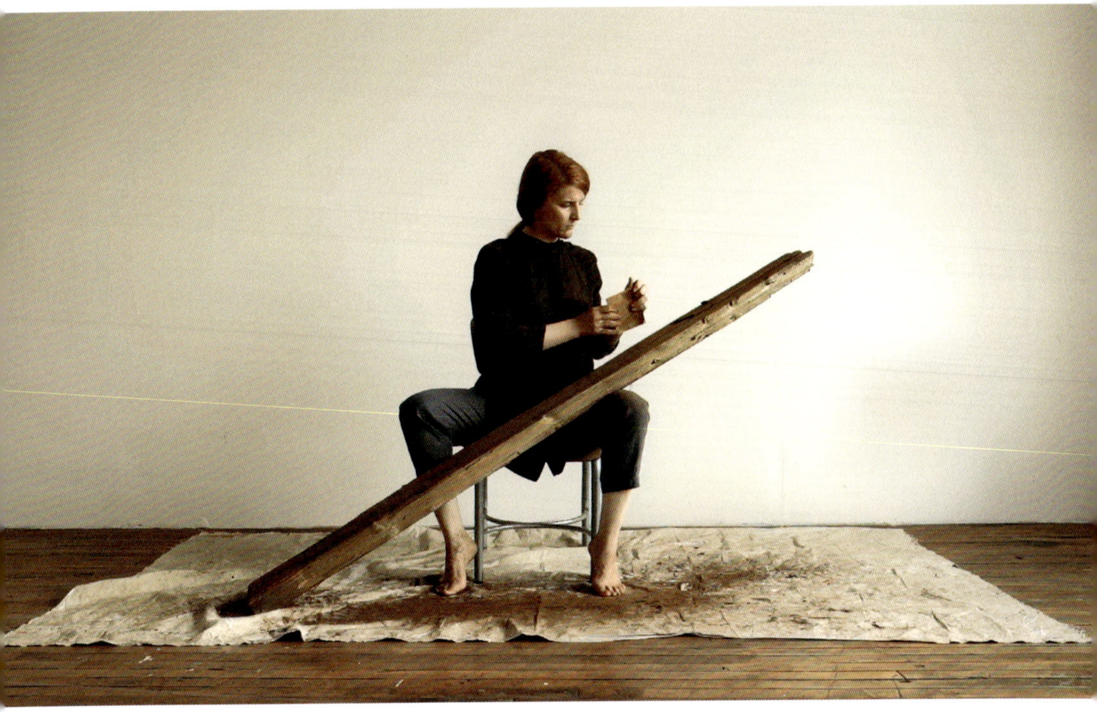

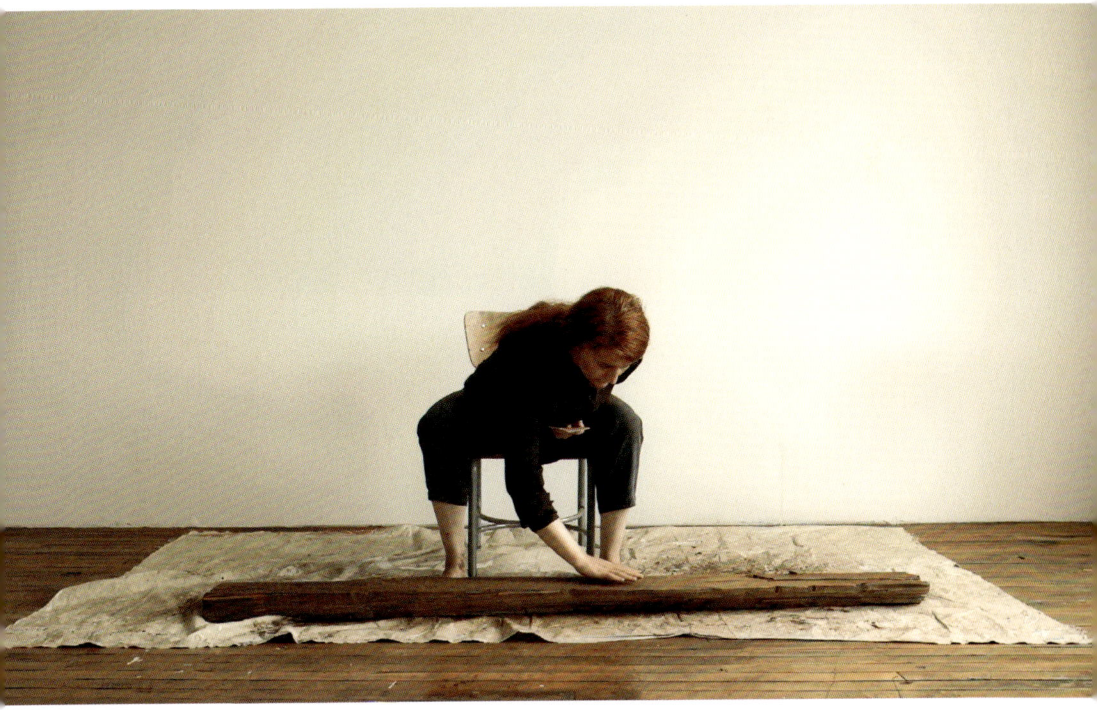

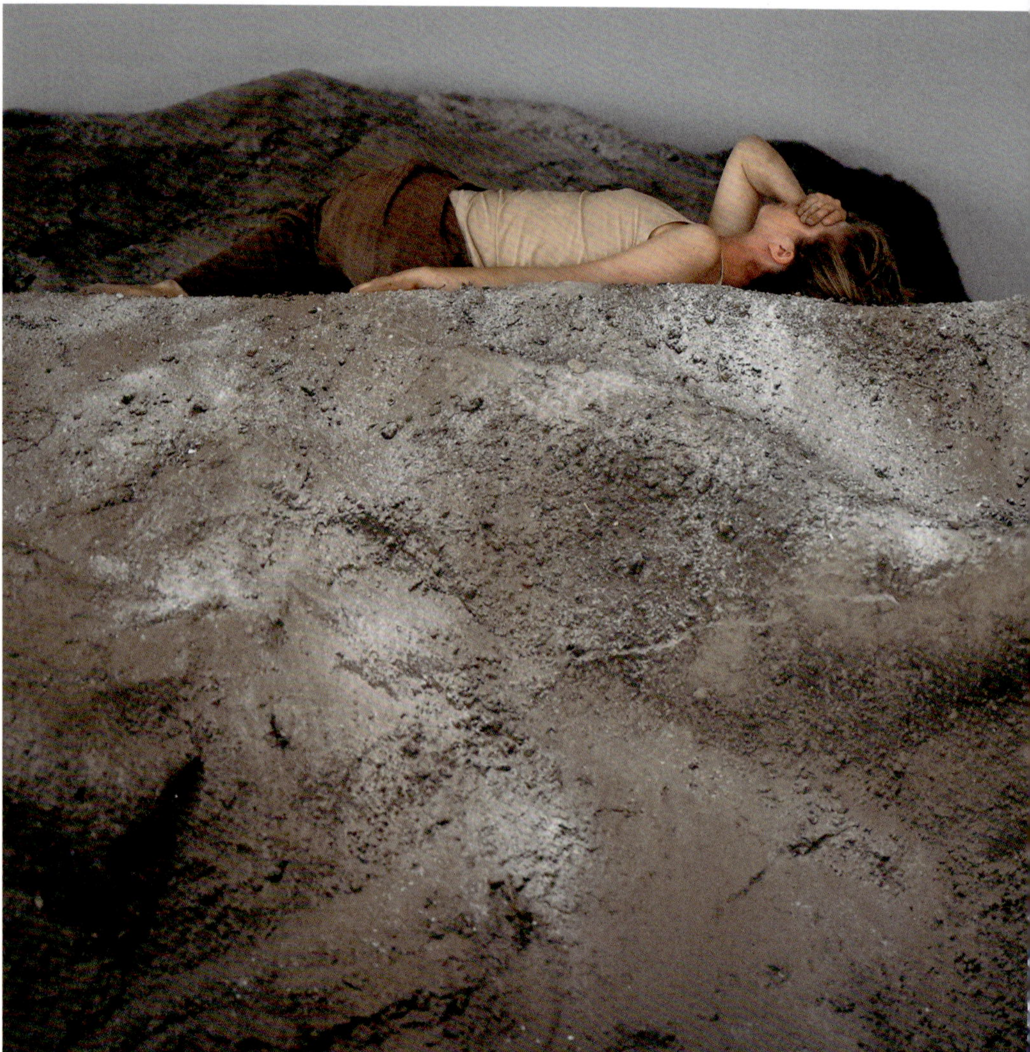

p. 94–97:

***The gift of sight***, 2022
Performance, dancer Caroline Beach
Project realized with the support of the Italian Council (2022)

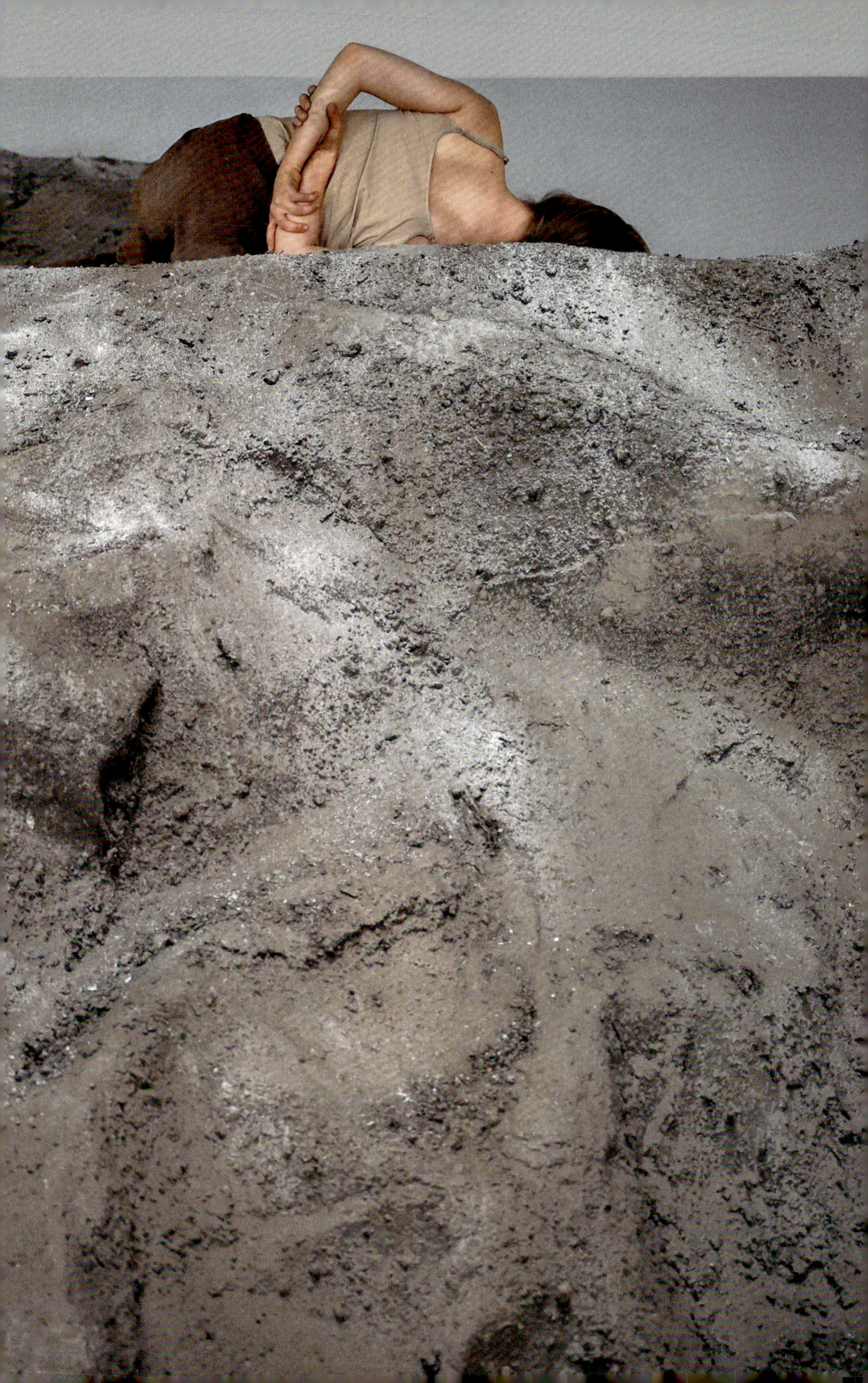

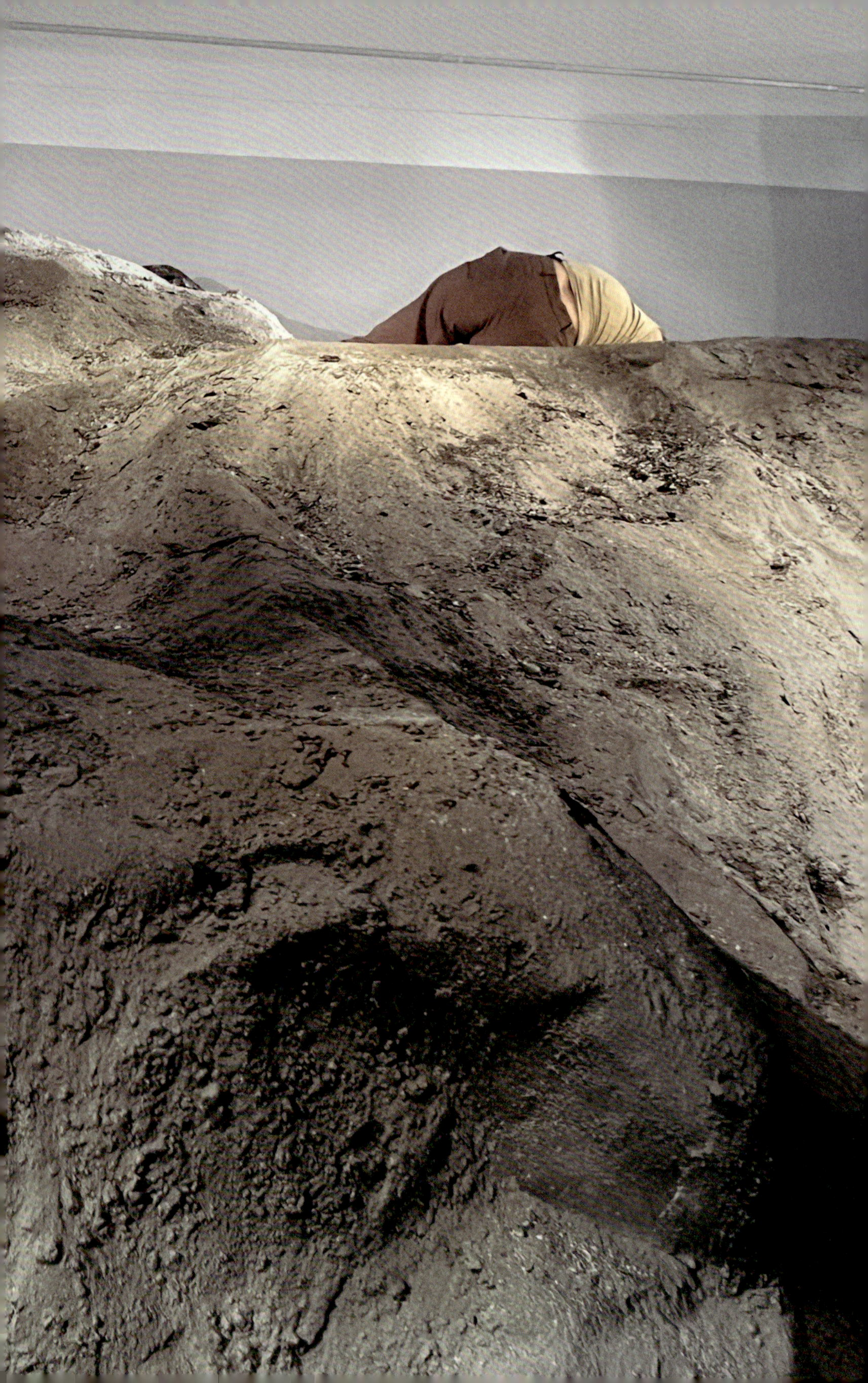

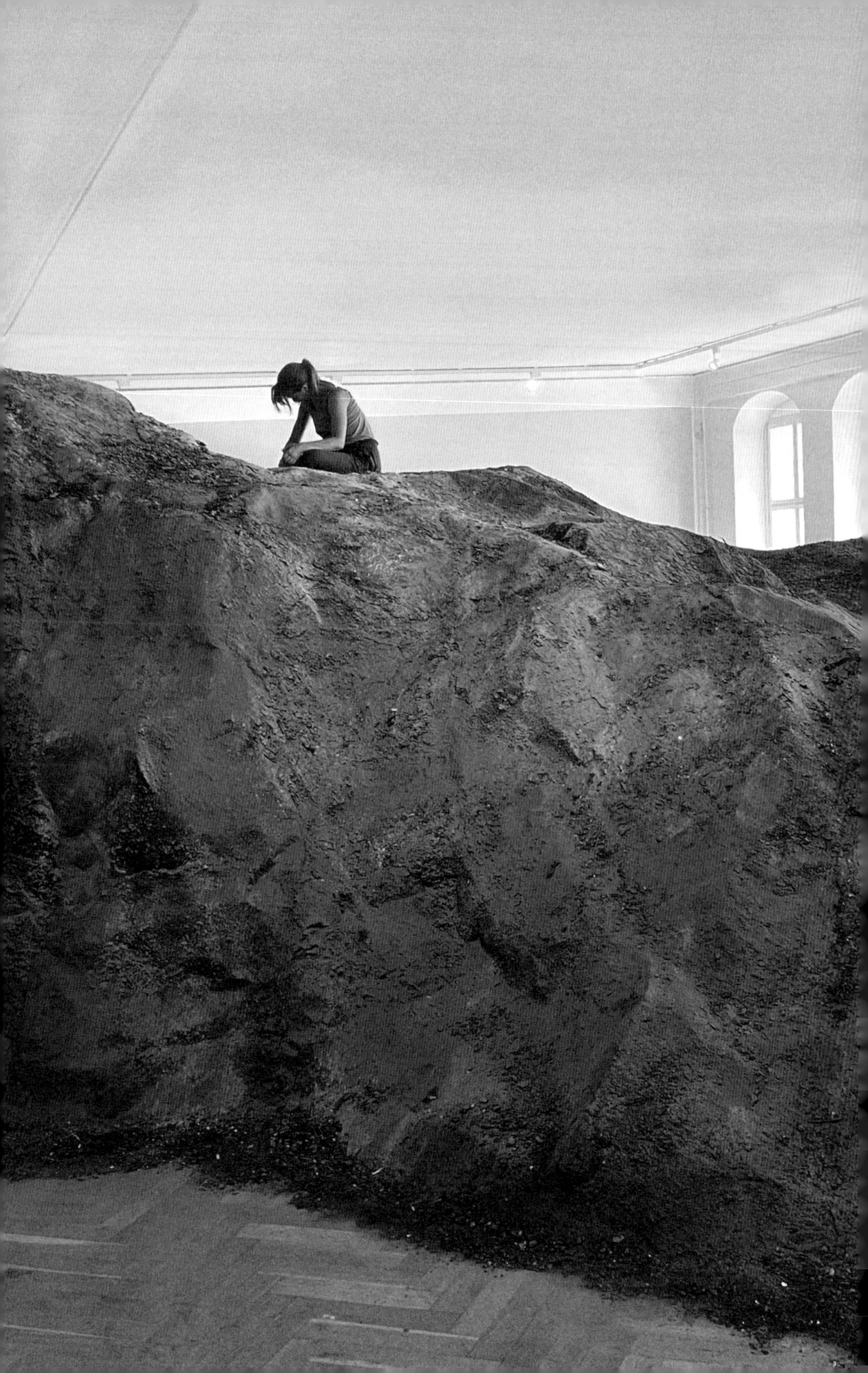

p. 26–27, 99–111:

***An interlude***, 2022
Living garden with approximately 100 plants, metal shelves
Dimensions variable
Project realized with the support of the Italian Council (2022)

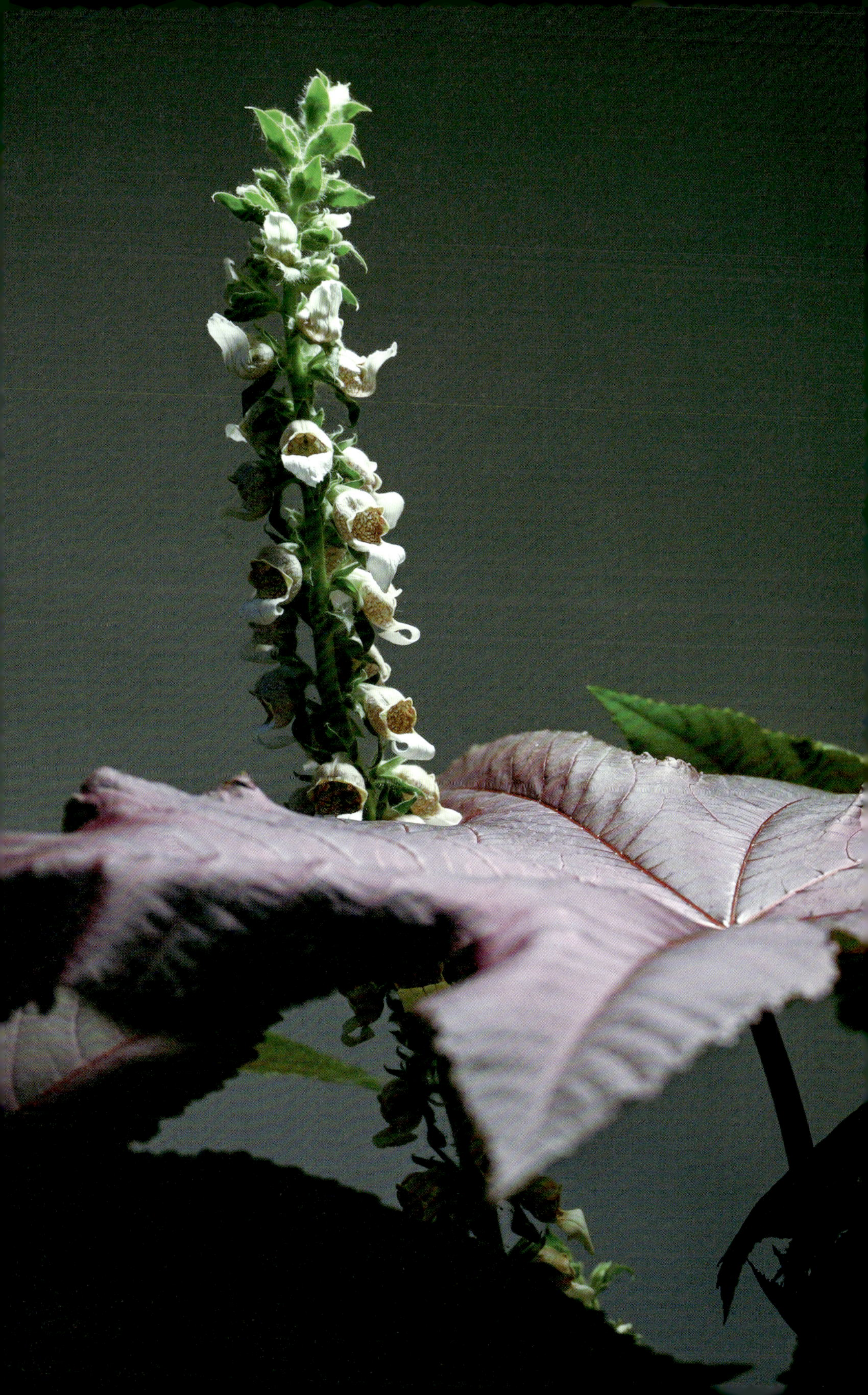

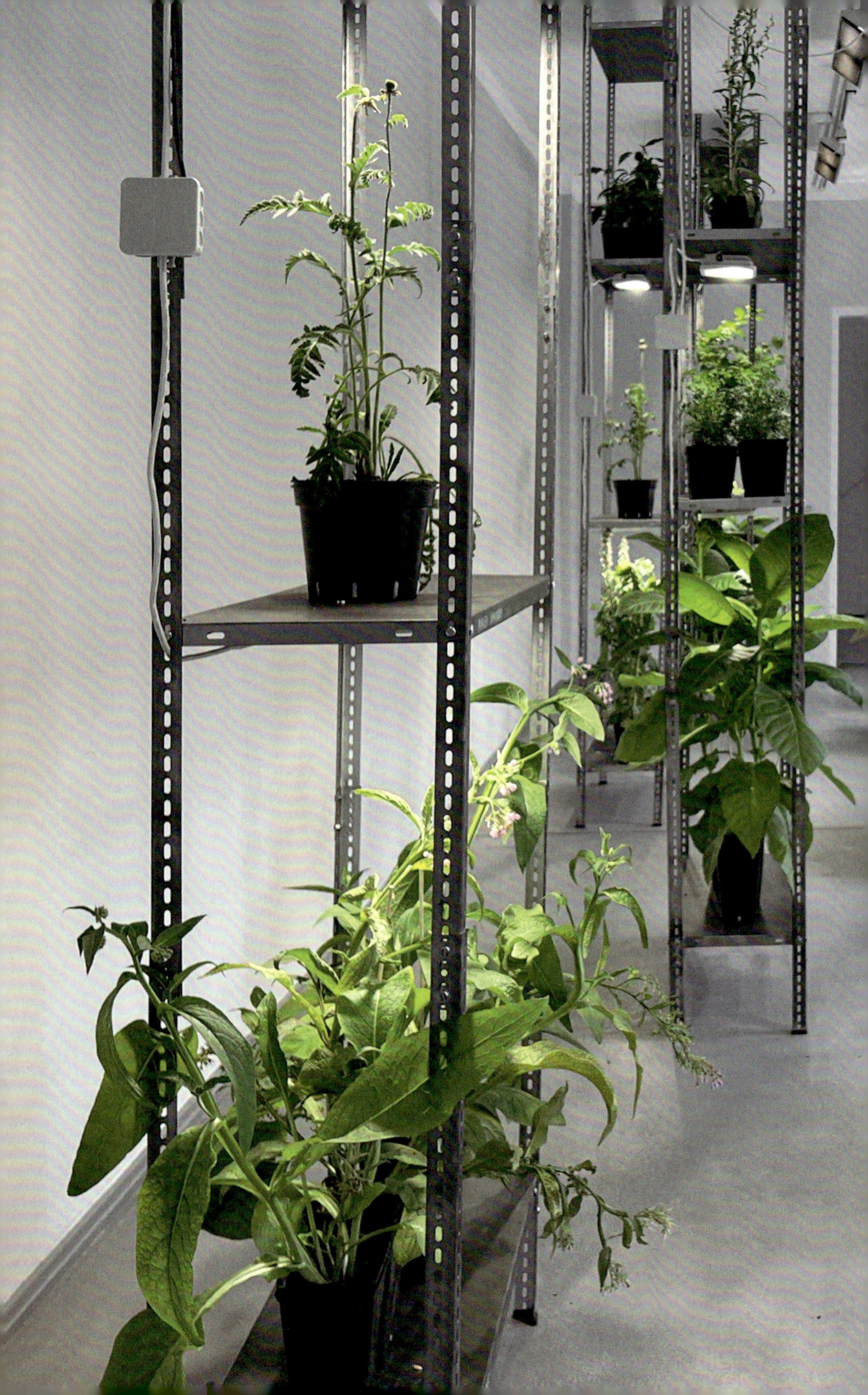

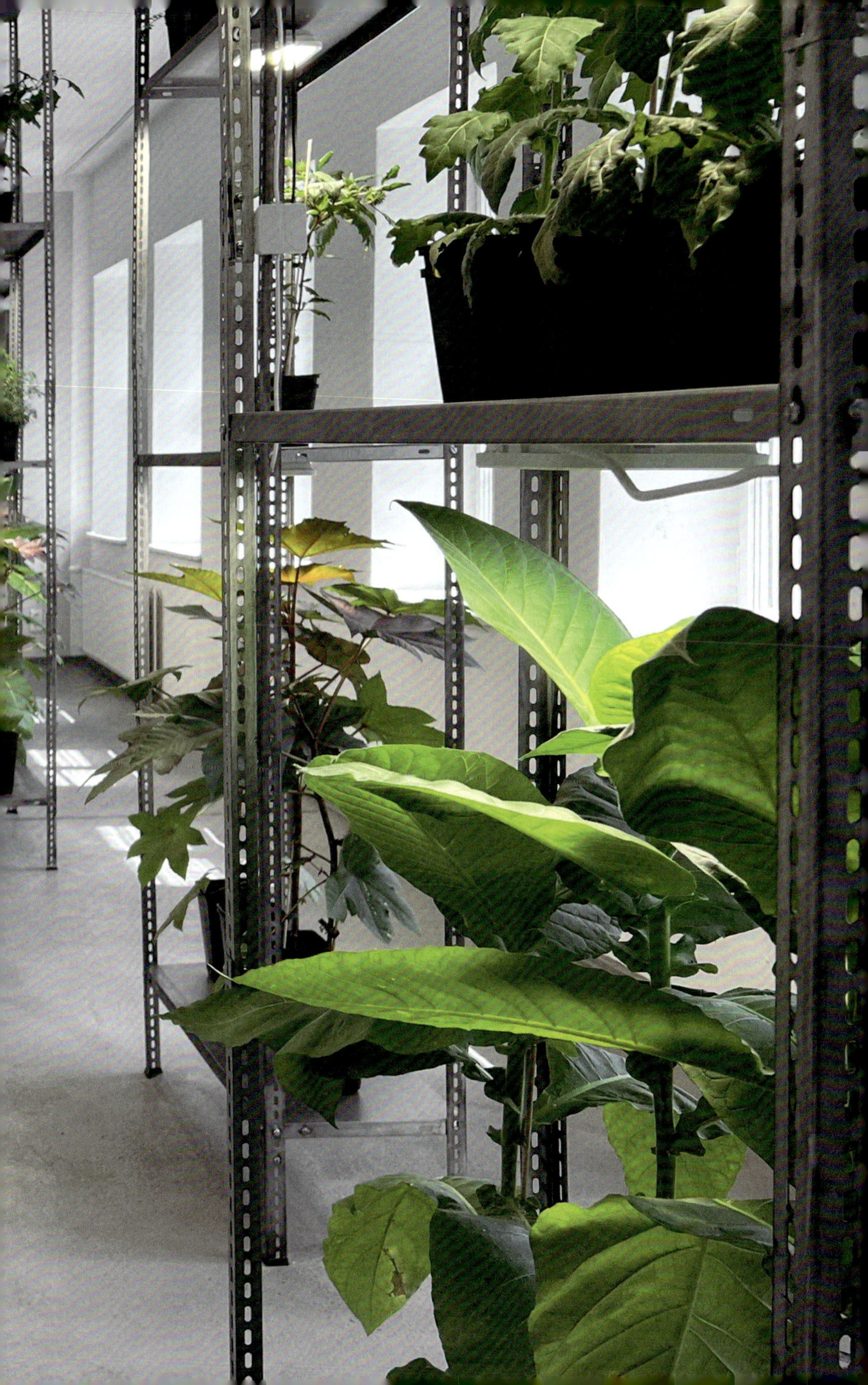

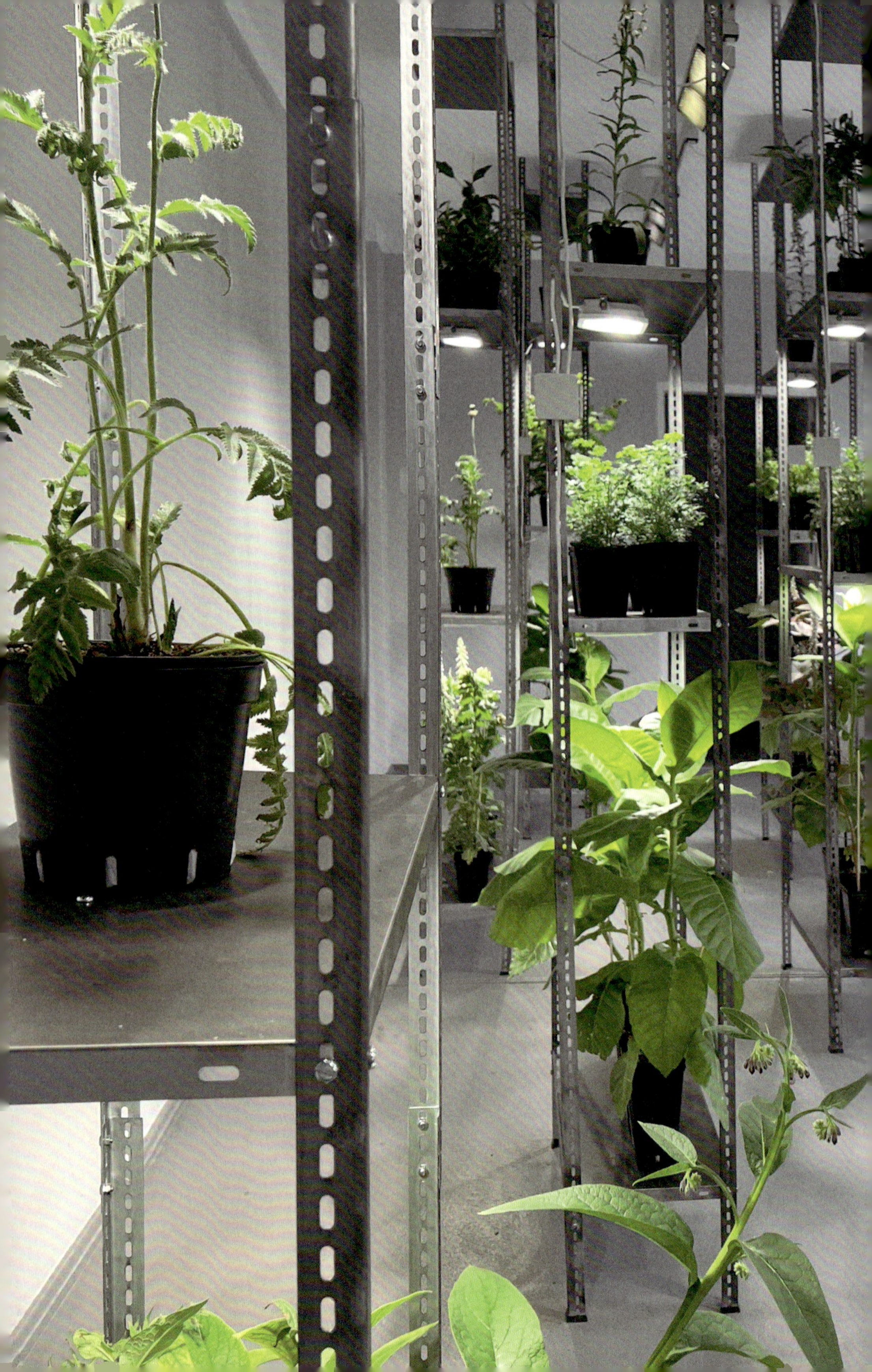

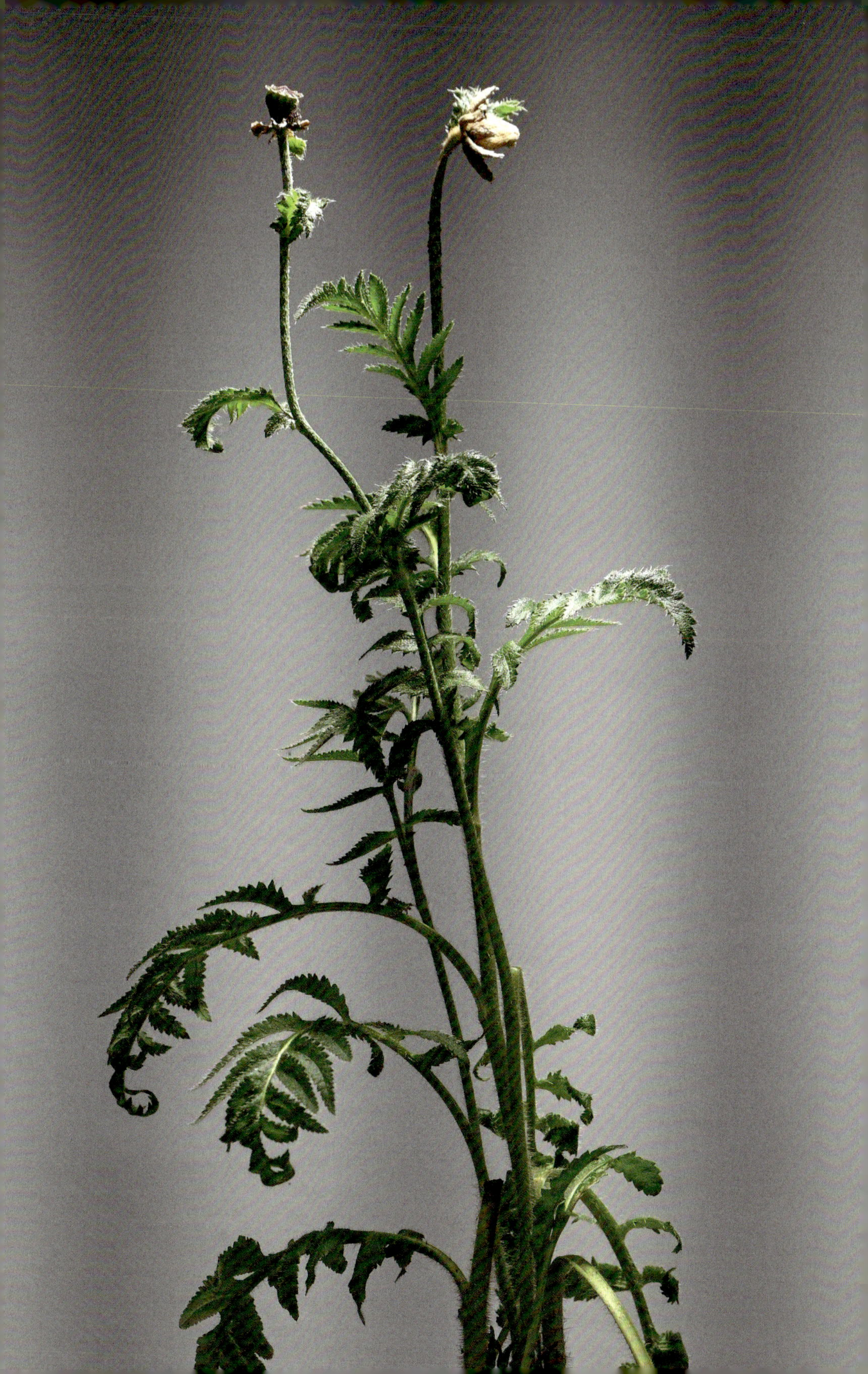

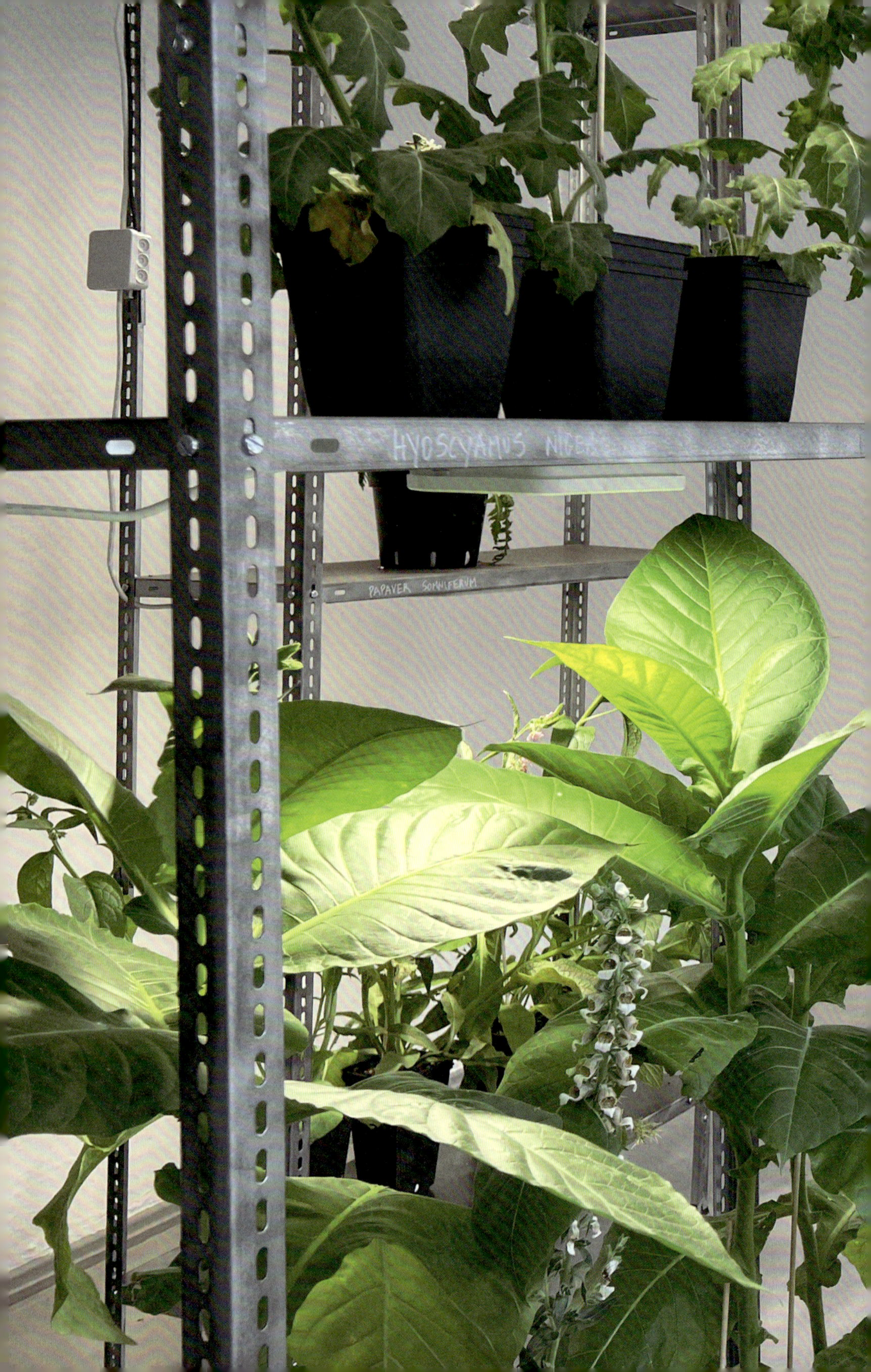
HYOSCYAMUS
PAPAVER SOMNIFERUM

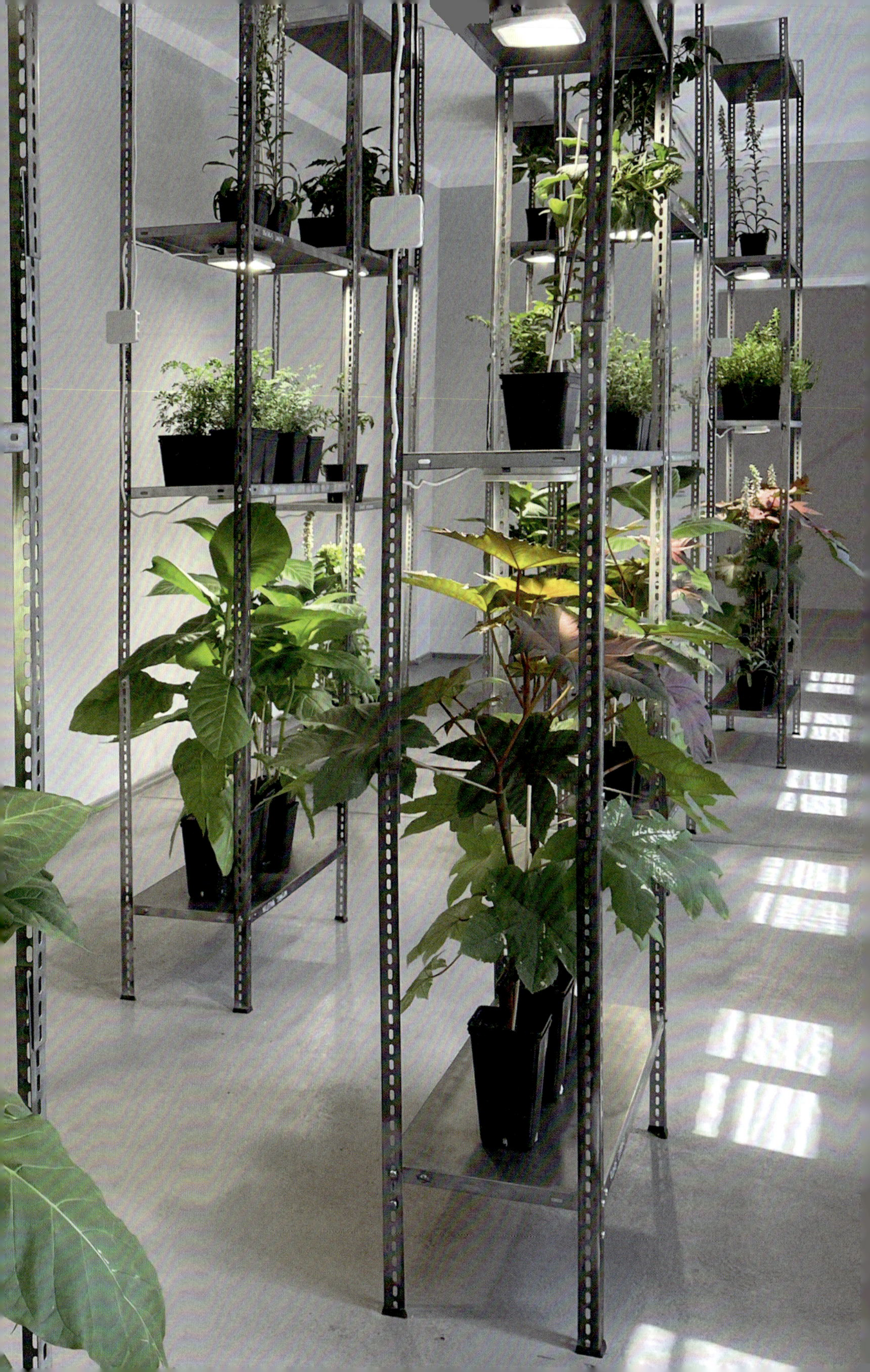

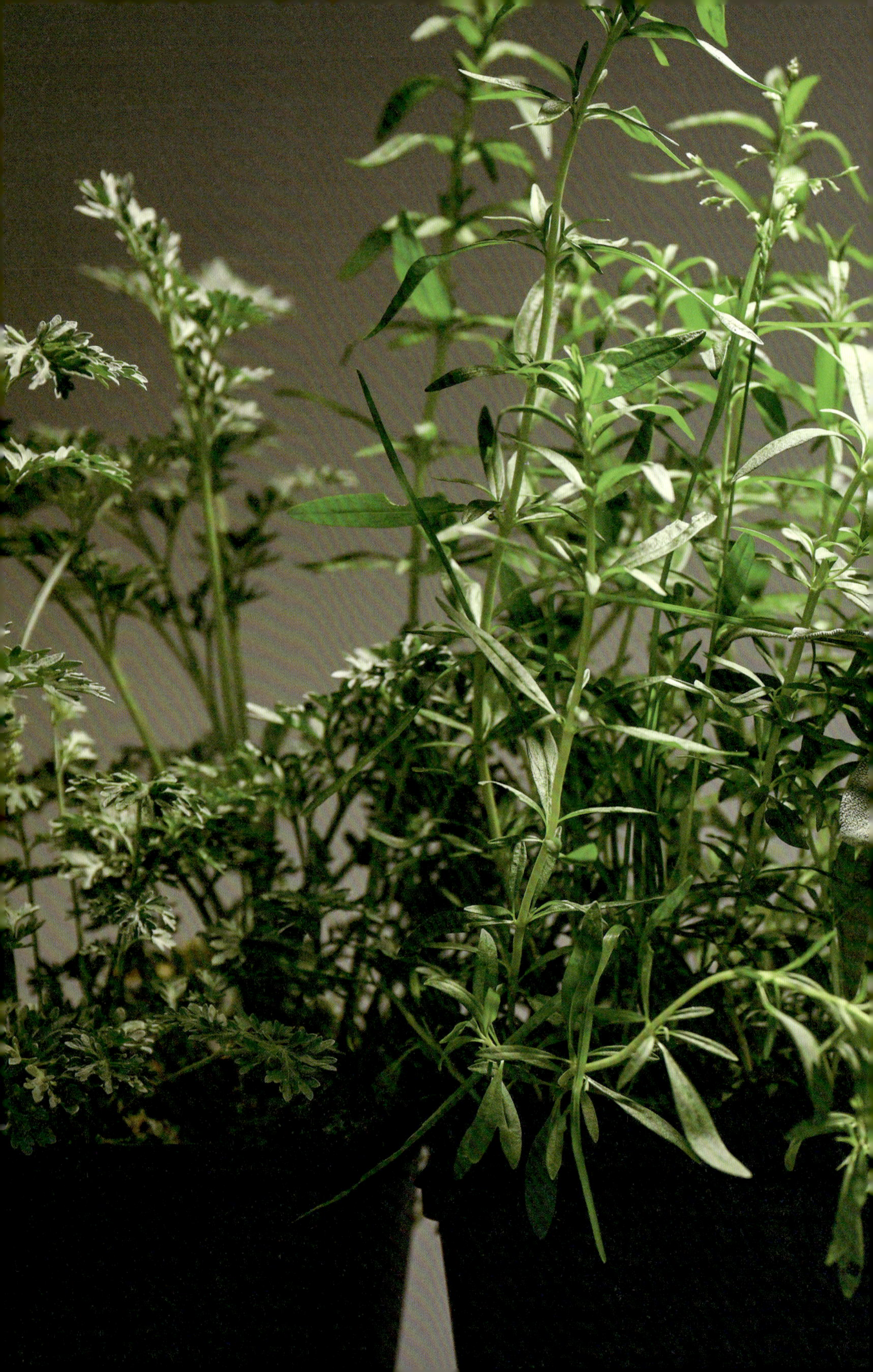

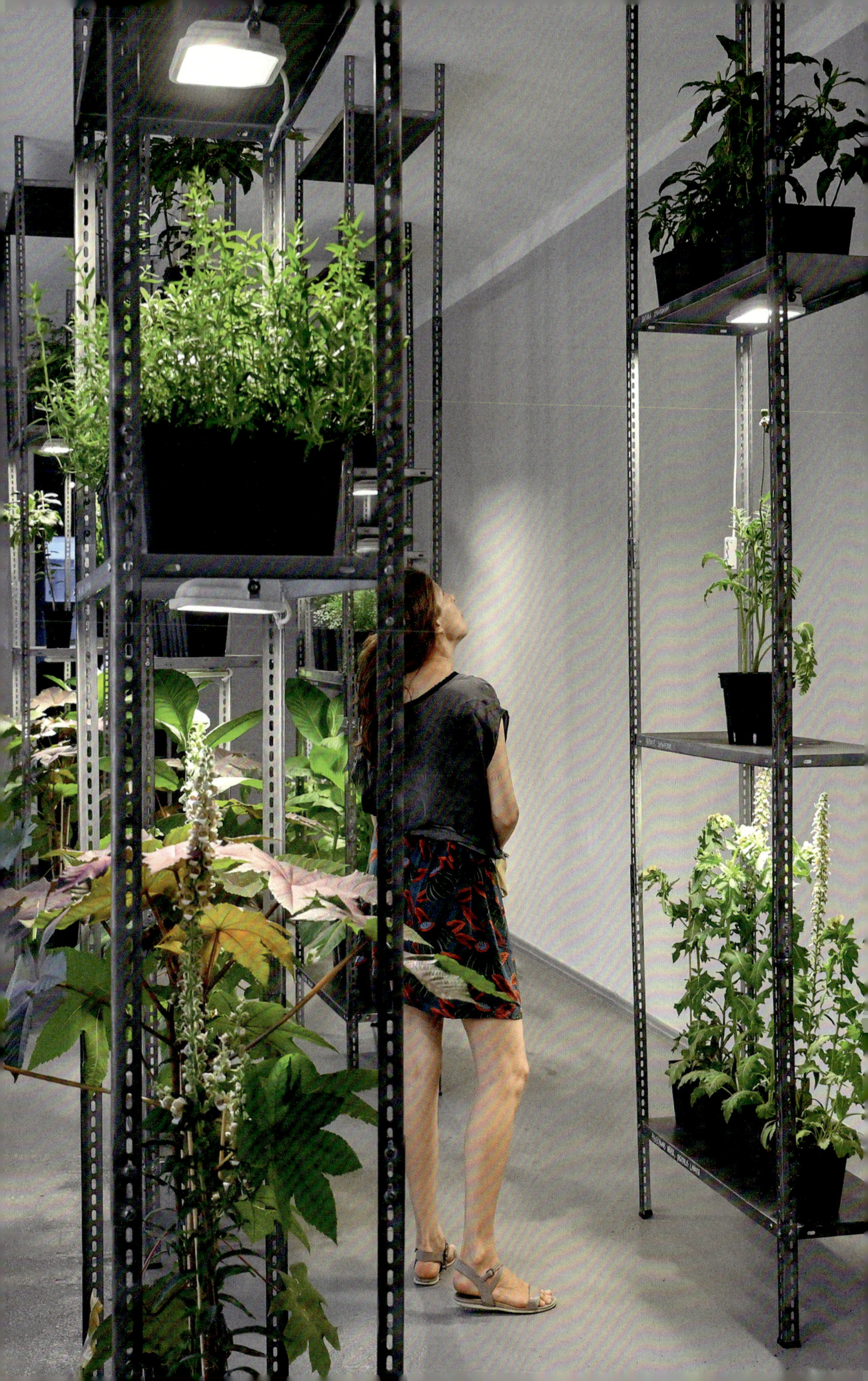

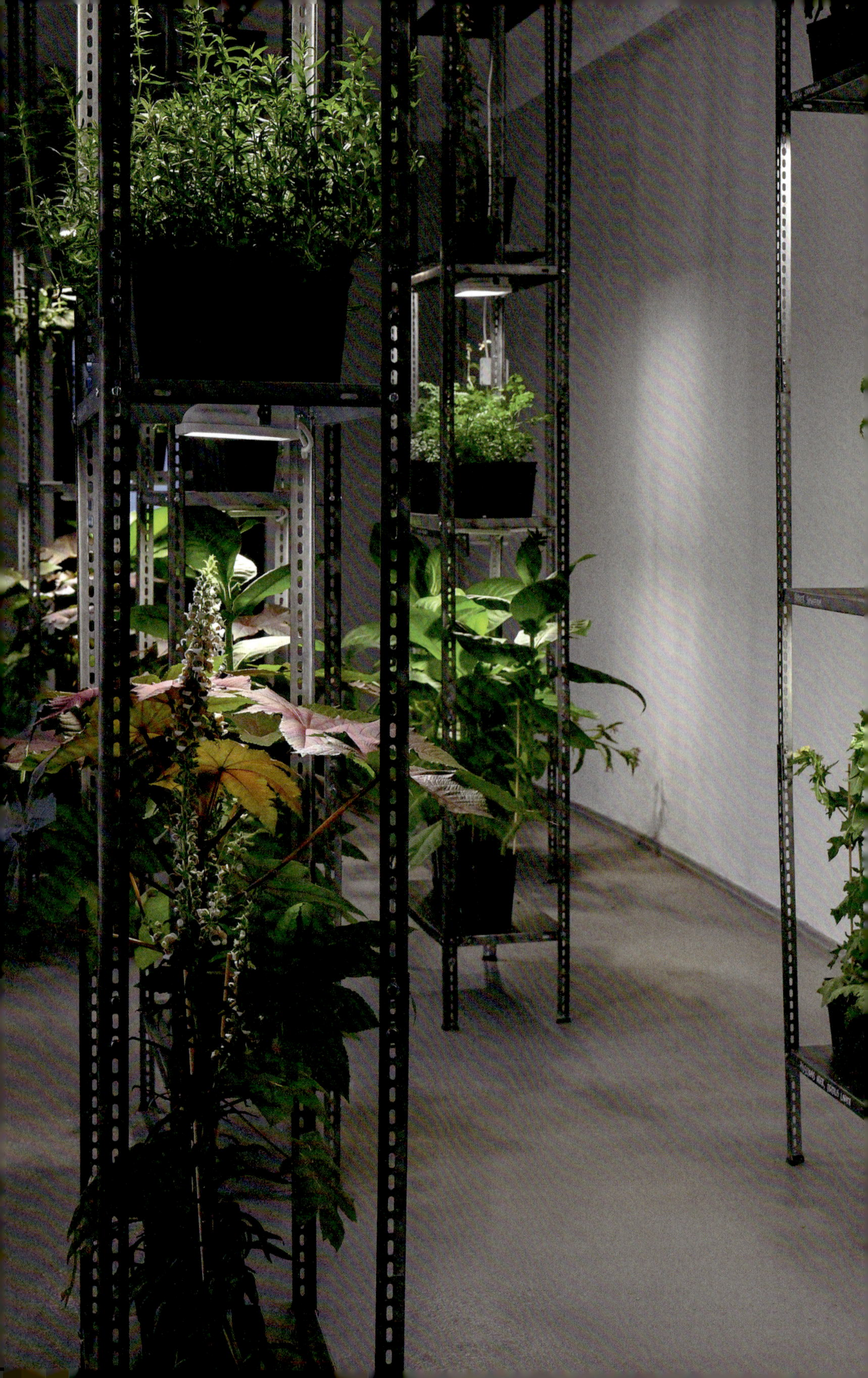

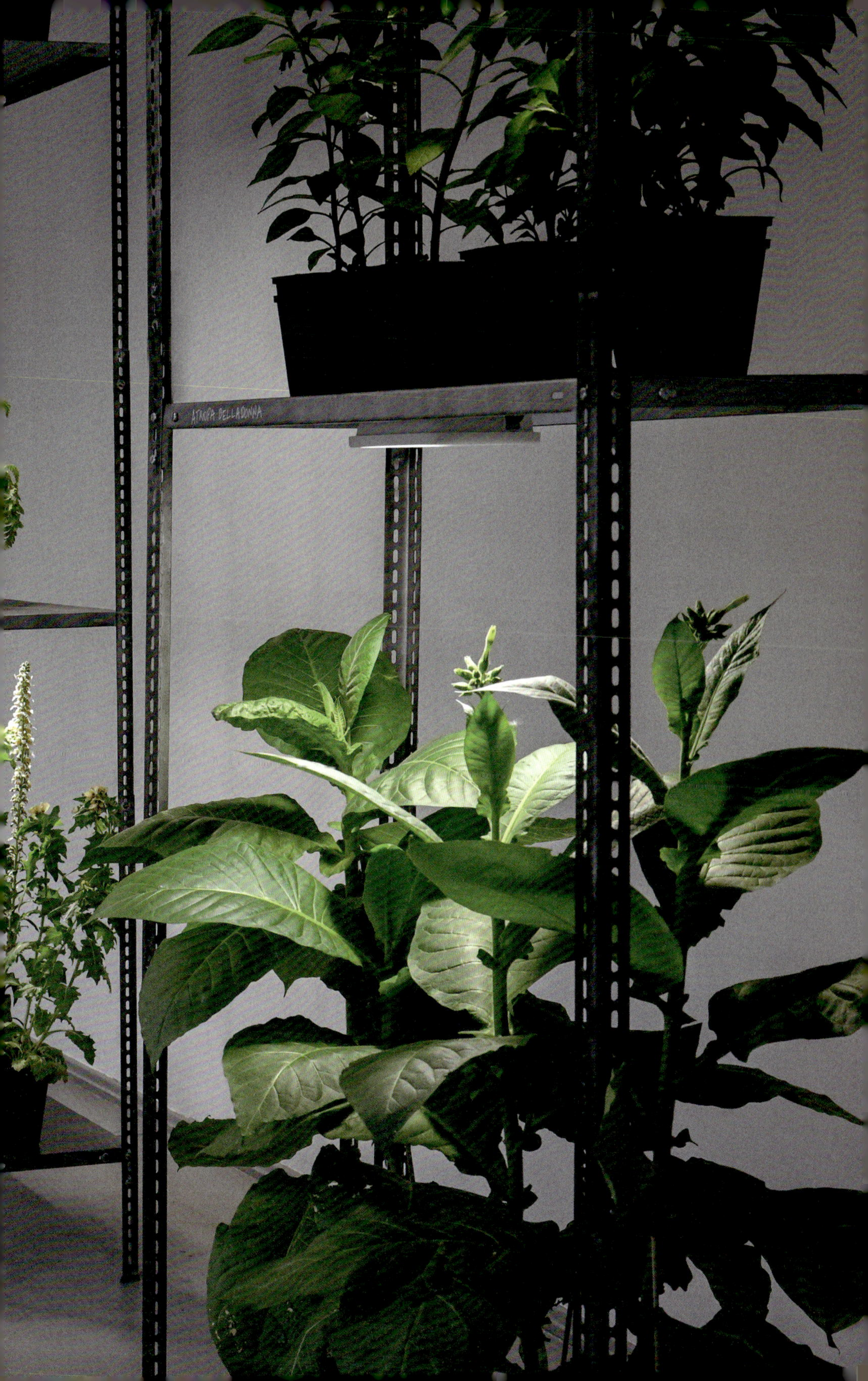
ATROPA BELLADONNA

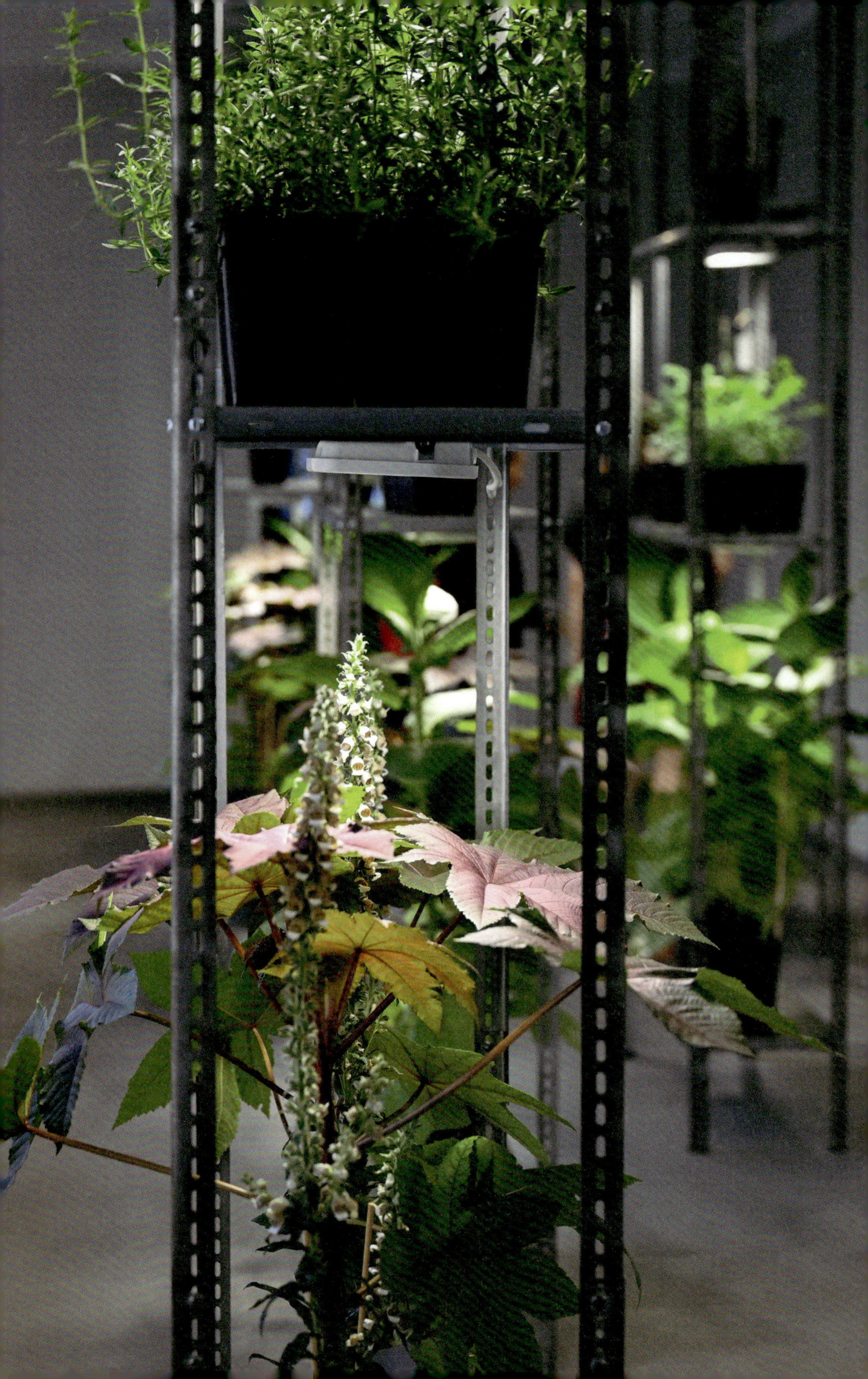

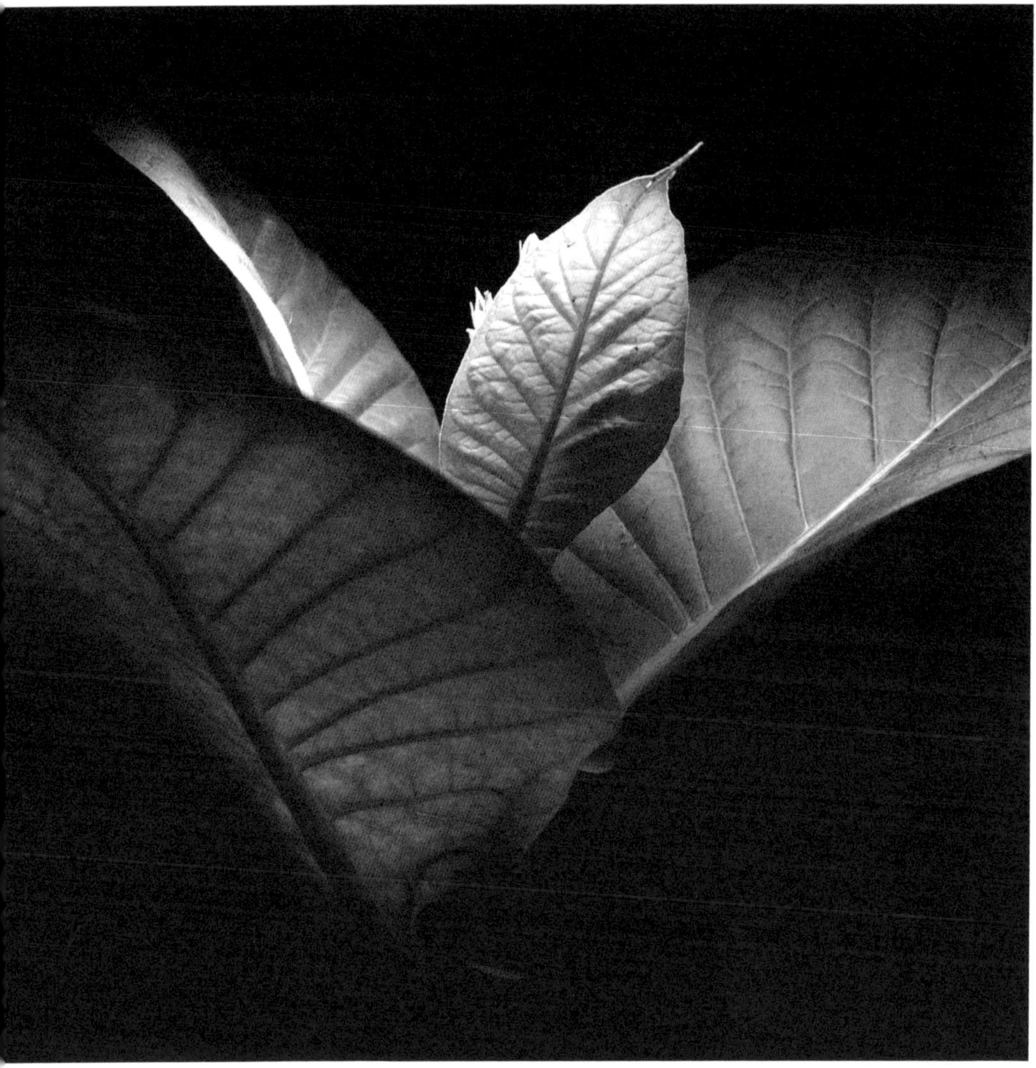

p. 26–27, 99–111:

***An interlude***, 2022
Living garden with approximately 100 plants, metal shelves
Dimensions variable
Project realized with the support of the Italian Council (2022)

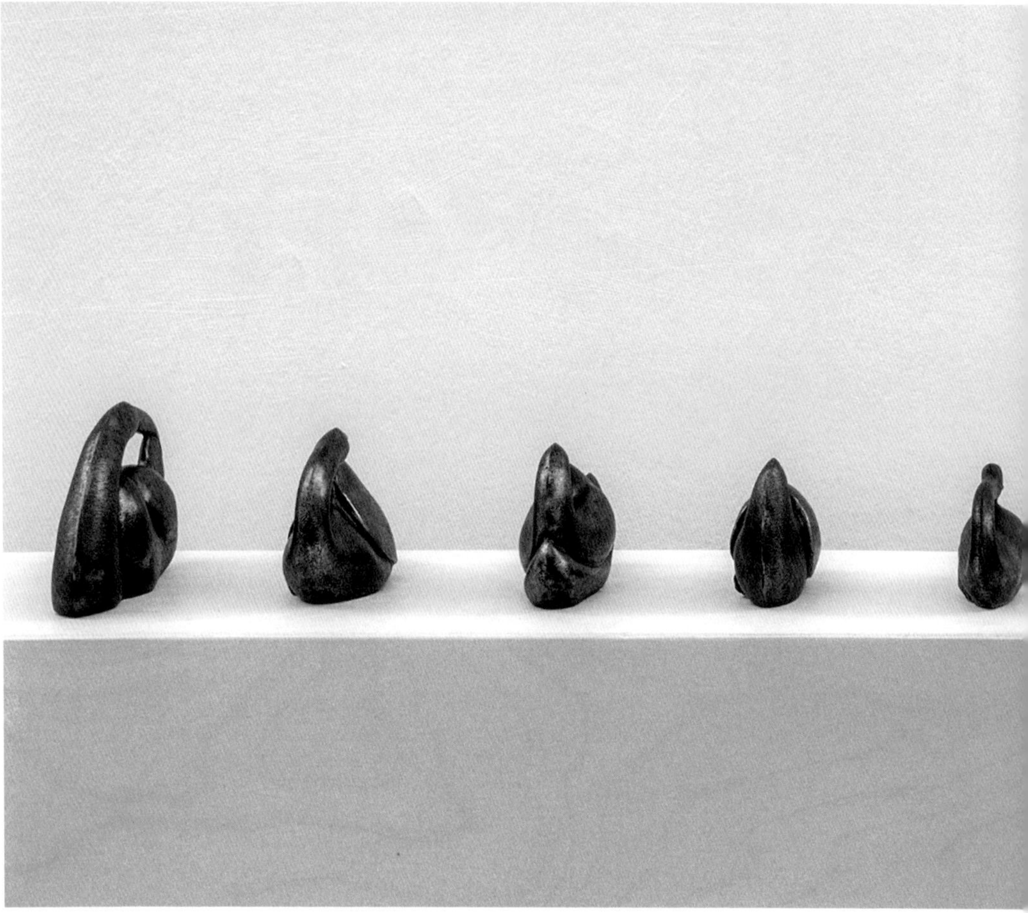

p. 112–119:

***Sum of the misdeeds and consents and cowardly acts***, 2022
Ten bronze sculptures, textiles, and wood
Dimensions variable
Project realized with the support of the Italian Council (2022)
[112–113: Installation view, *In Prestissimo*,
Peola Simondi Gallery, Italy, 2022]

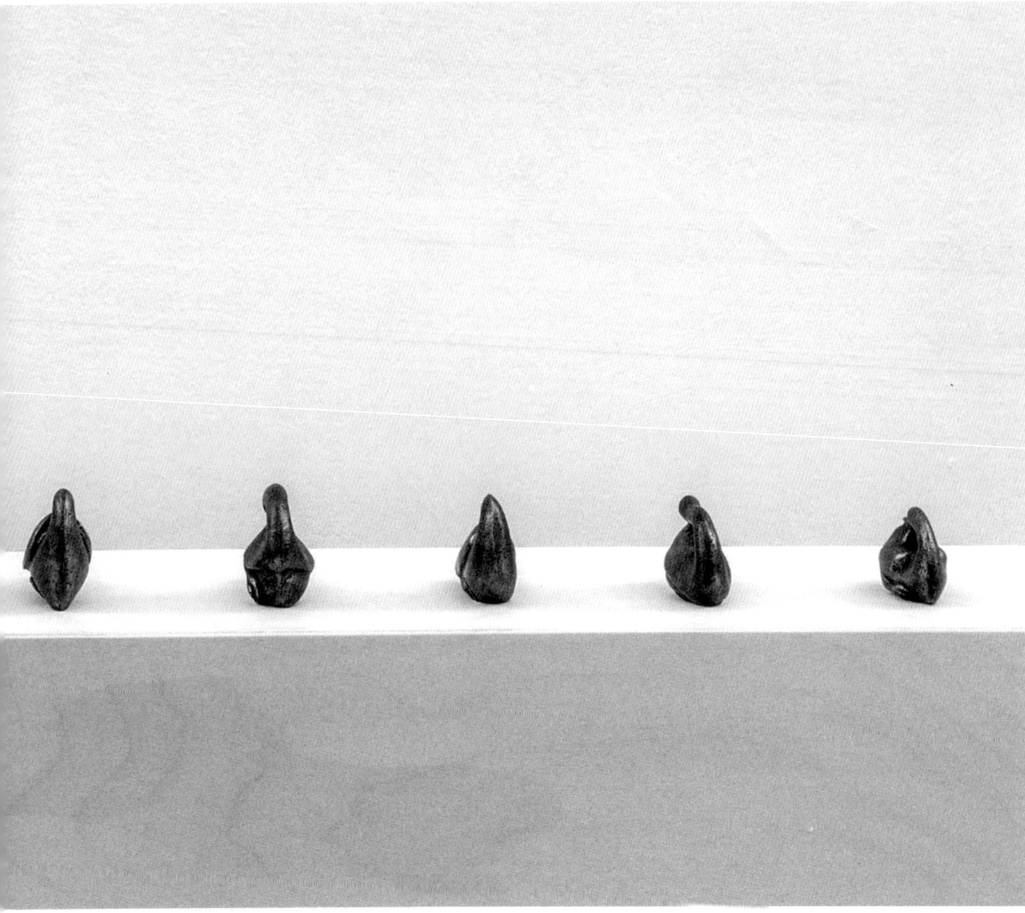

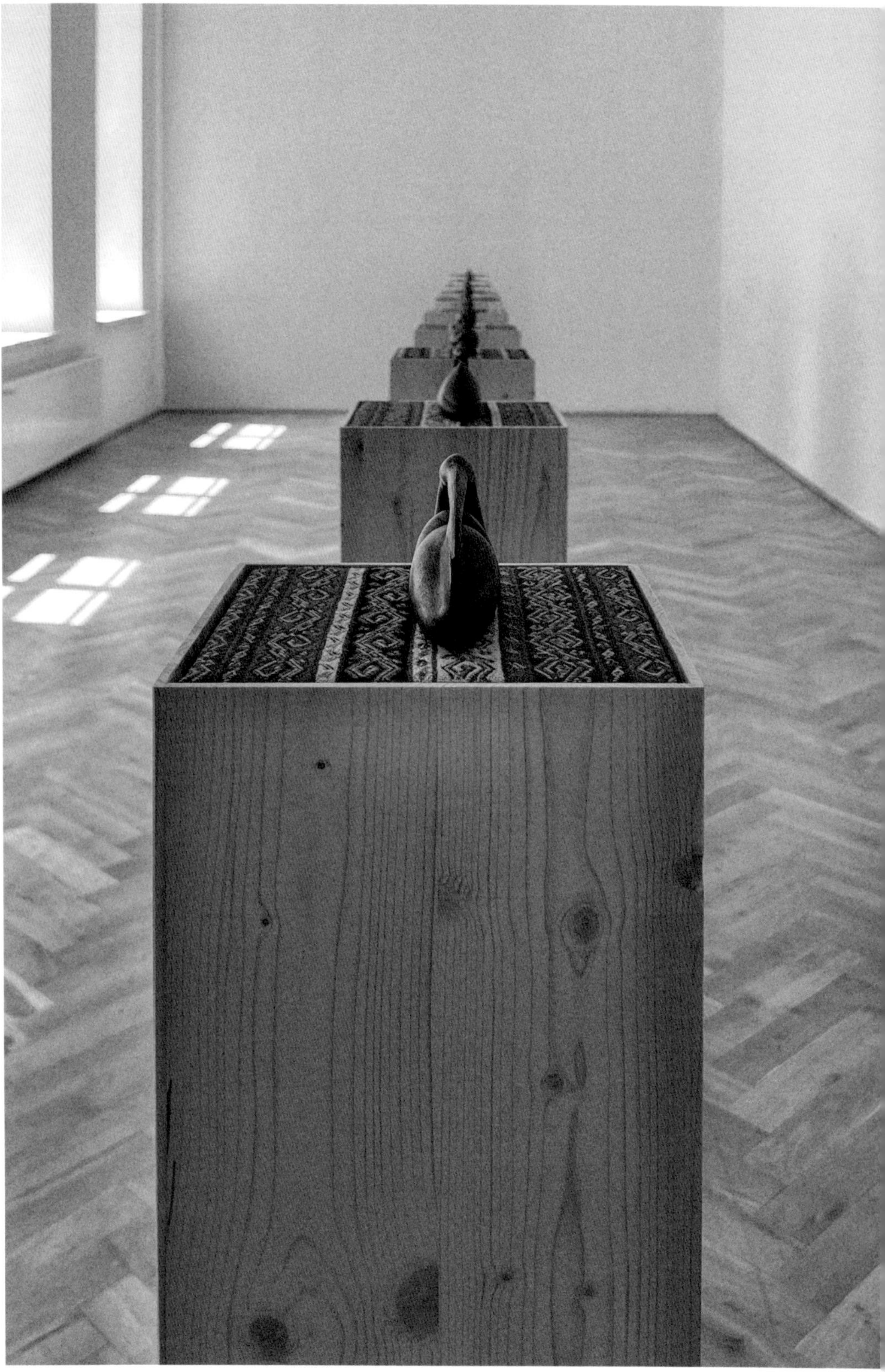

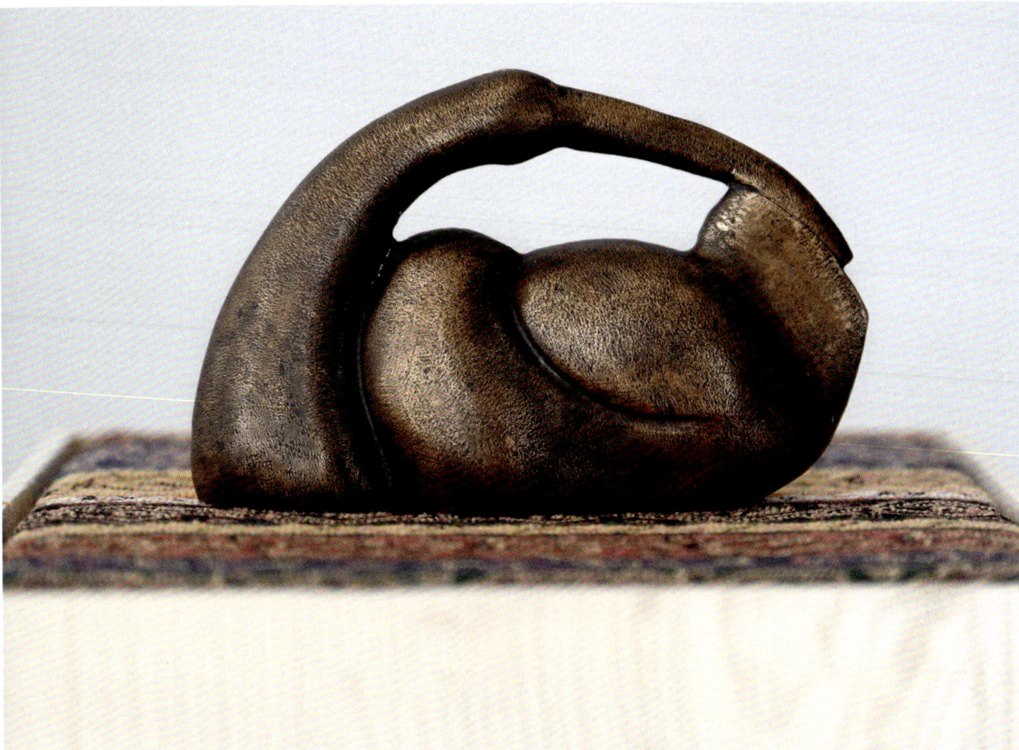

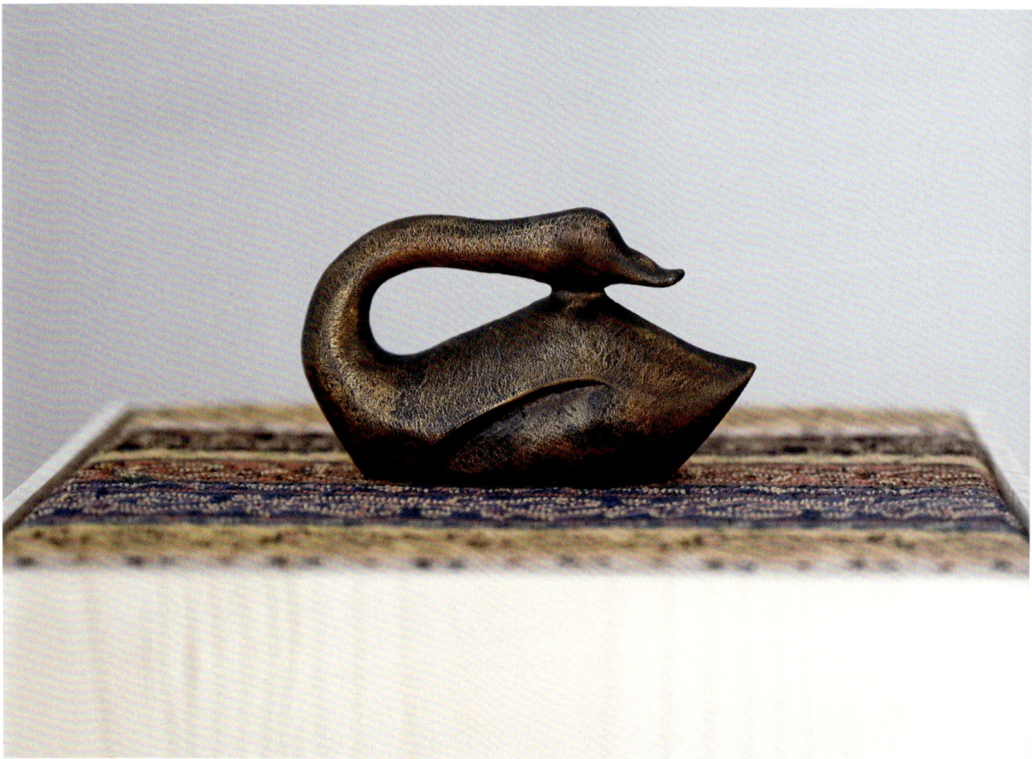

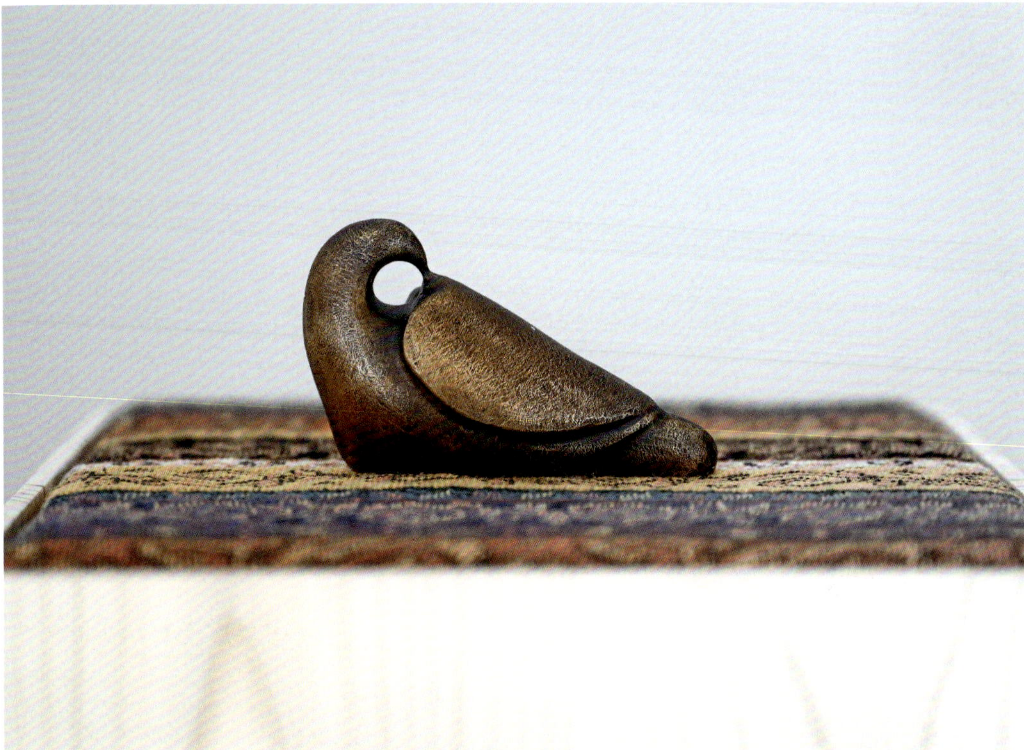

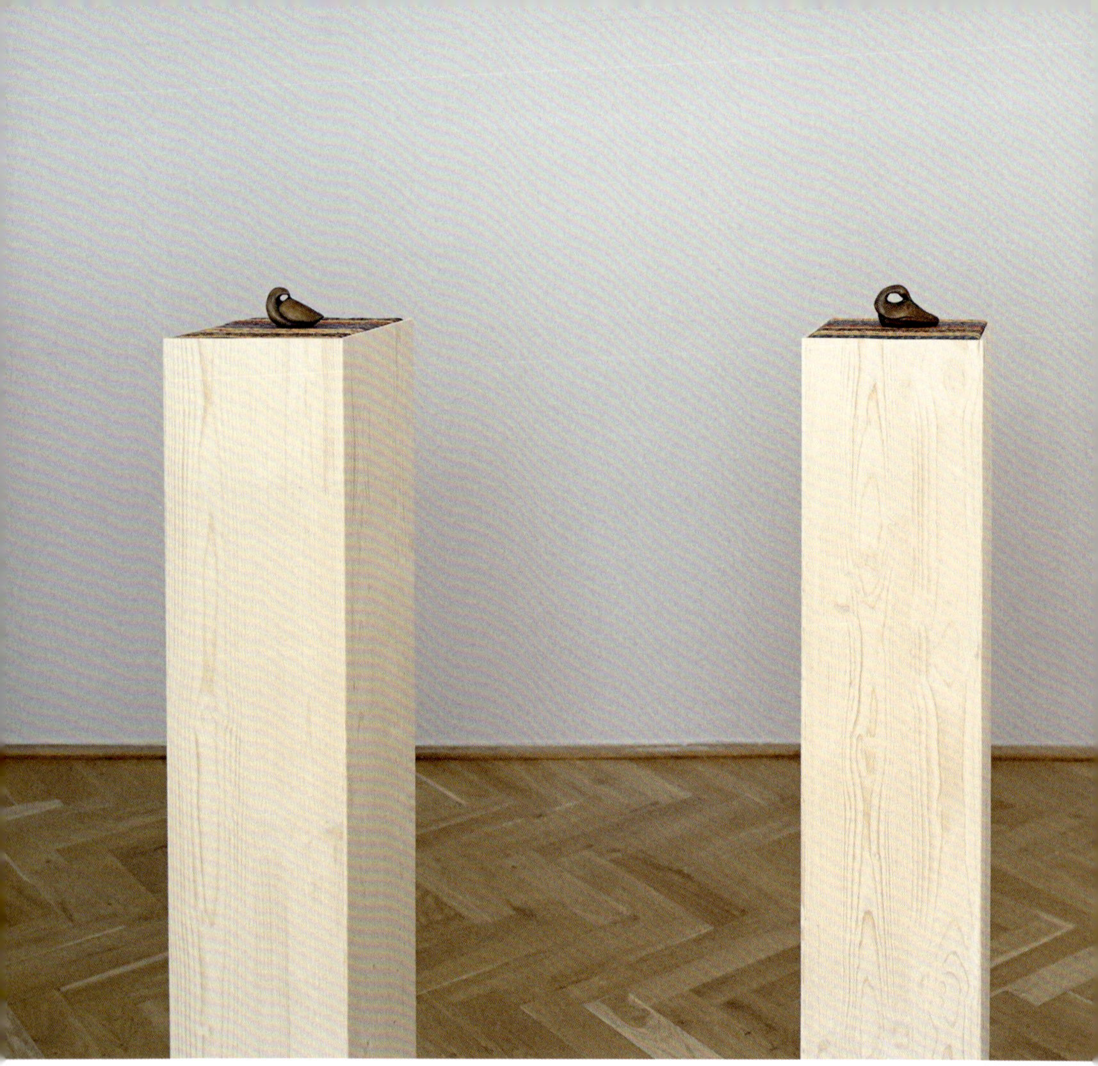

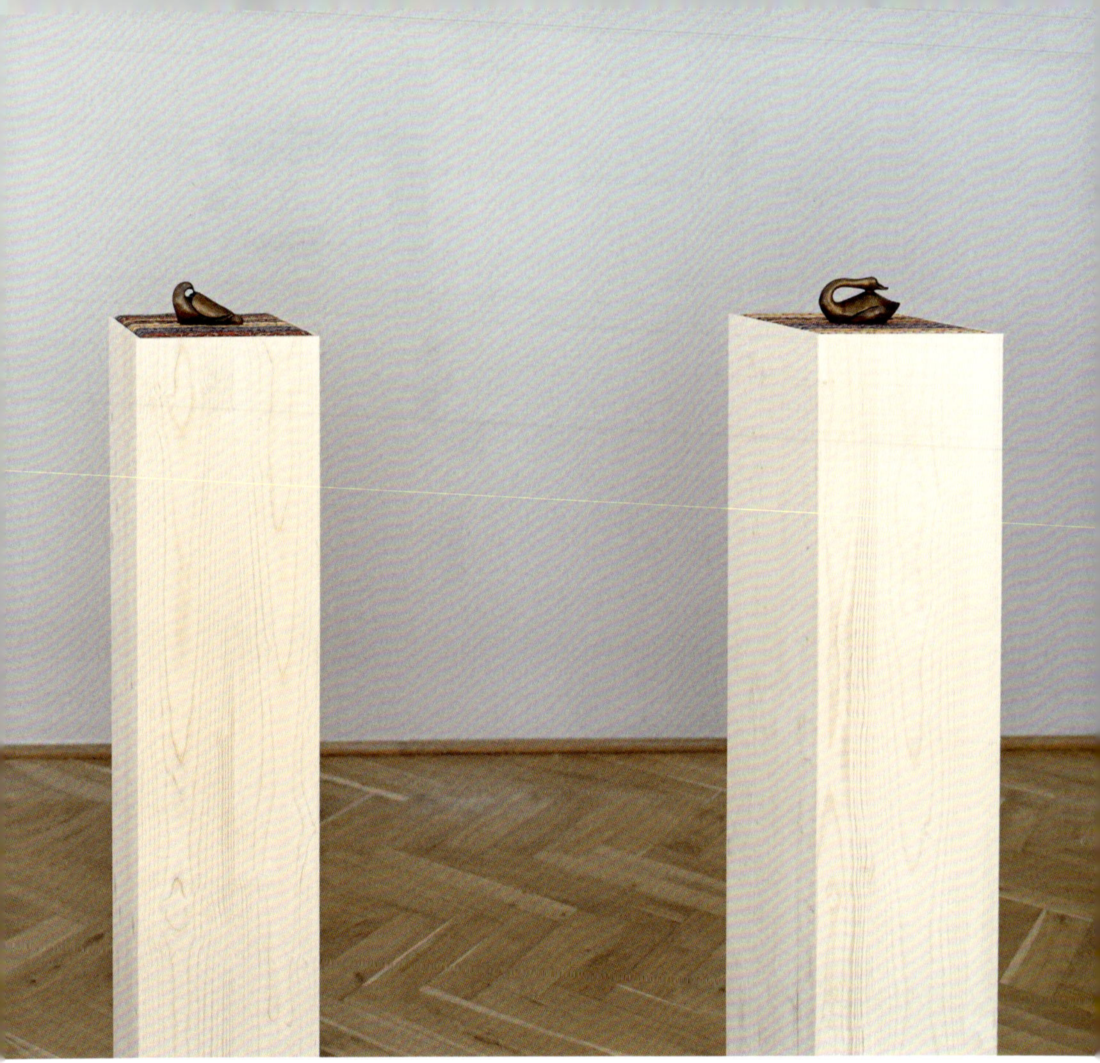

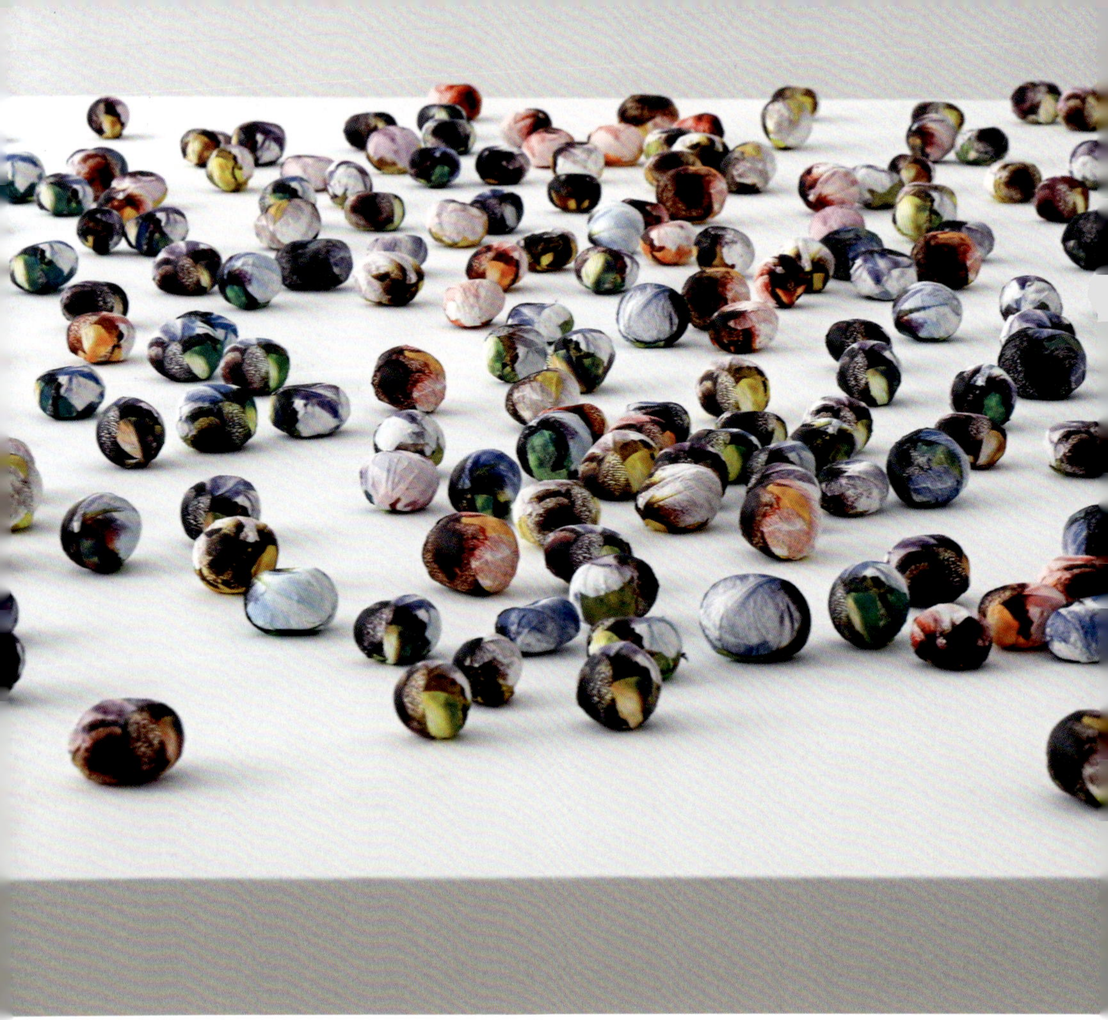

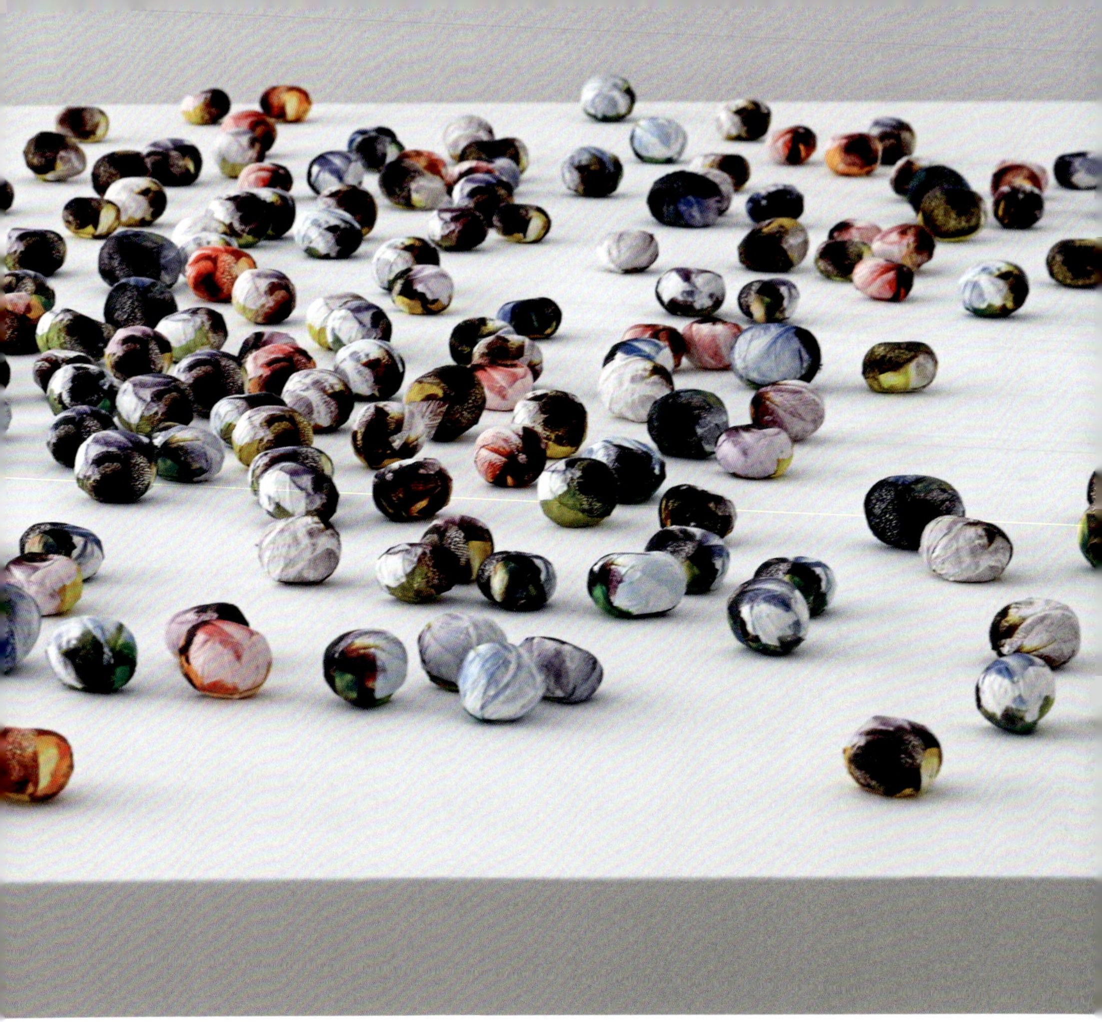

p. 120–126:

***Perpetual lure and insistent fear***, 2022
350 screen prints (monotypes)

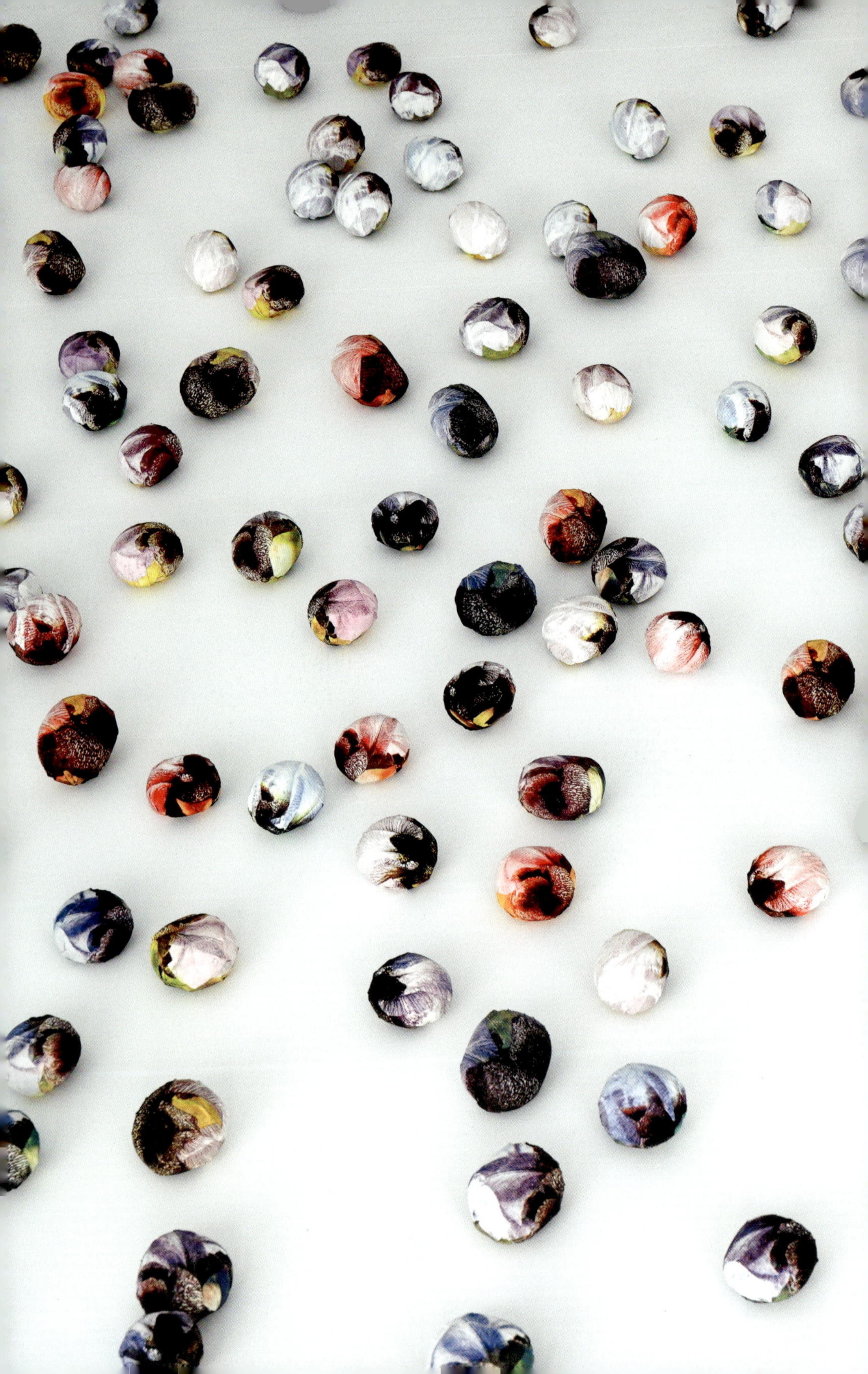

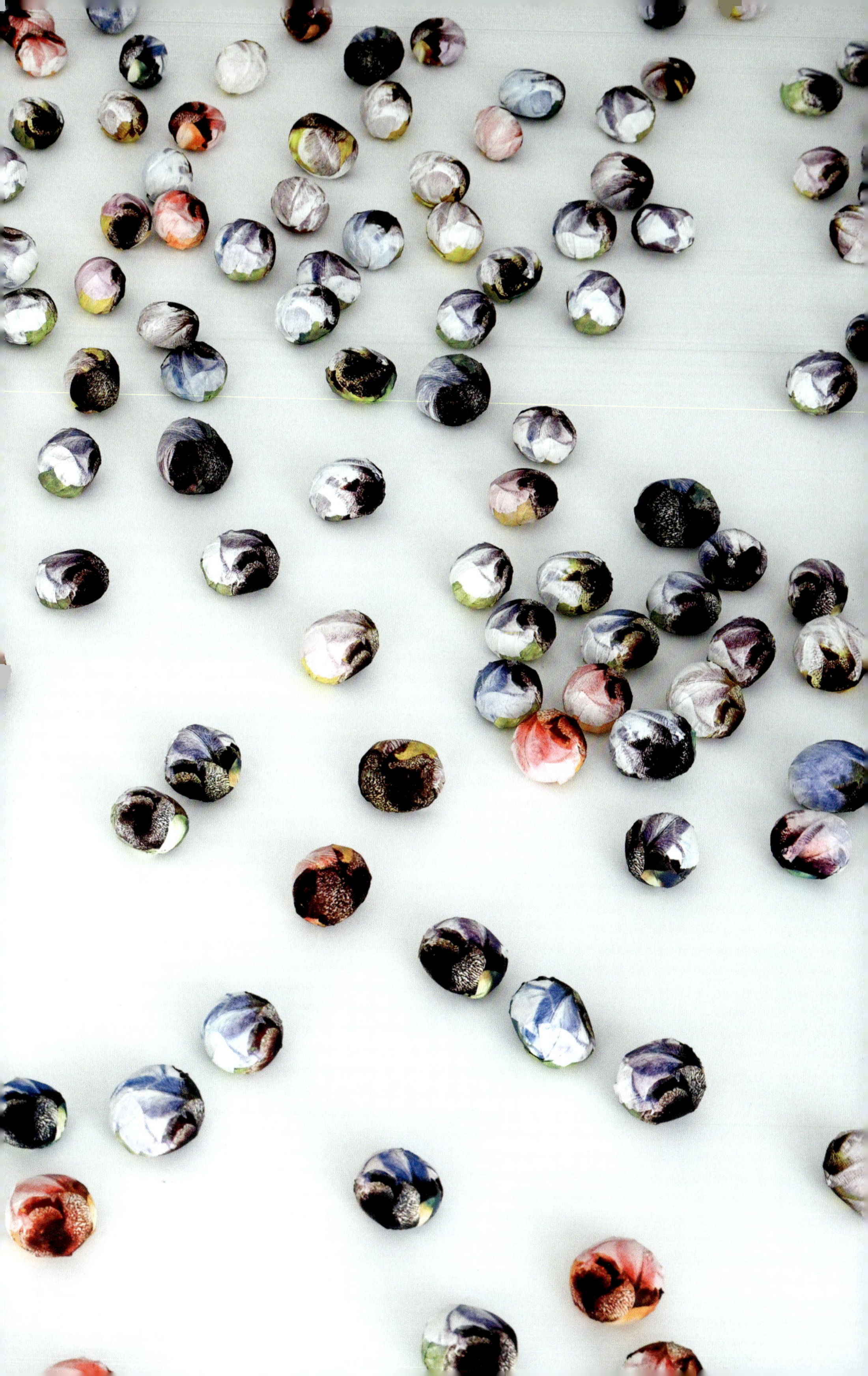

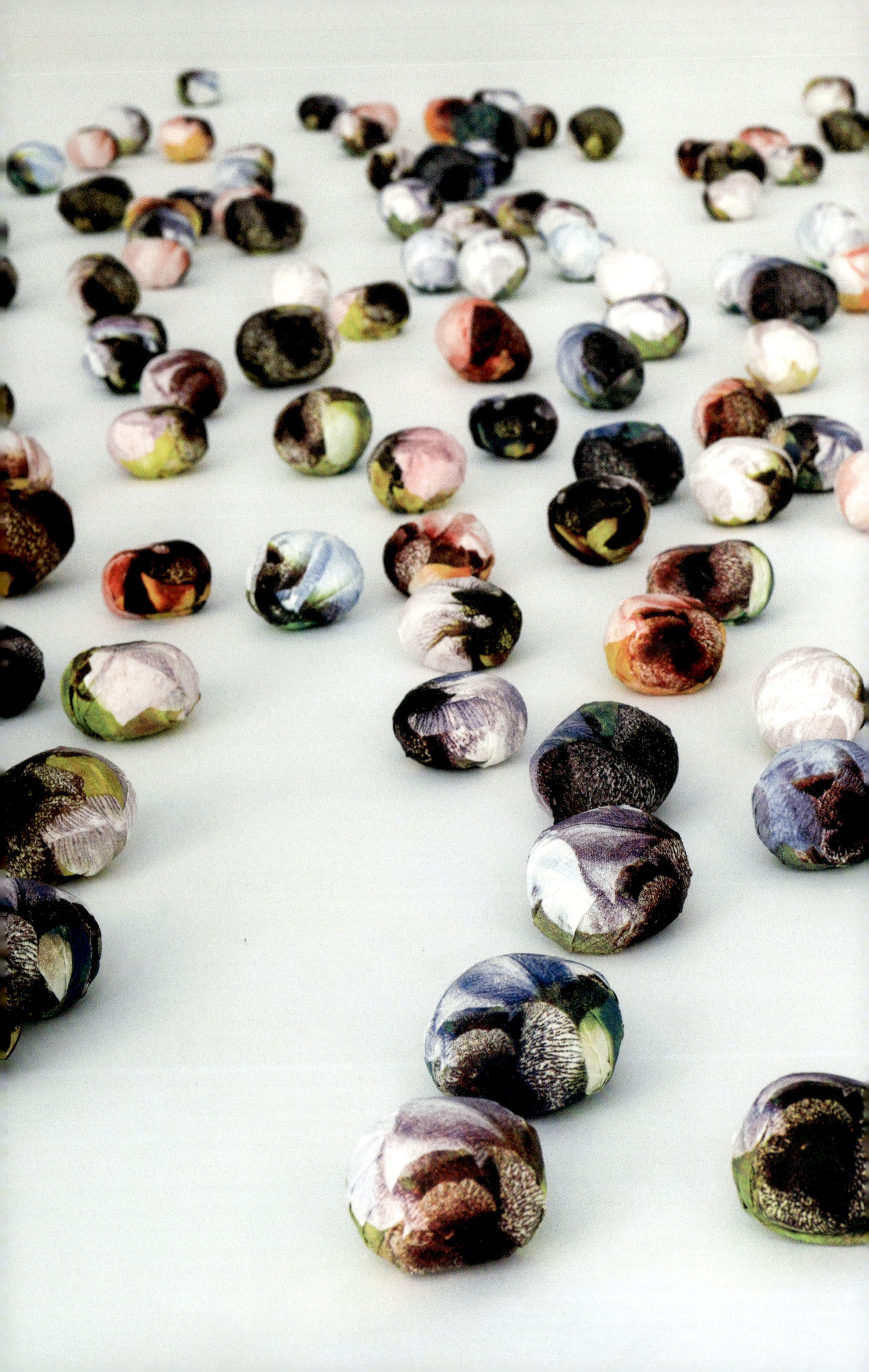

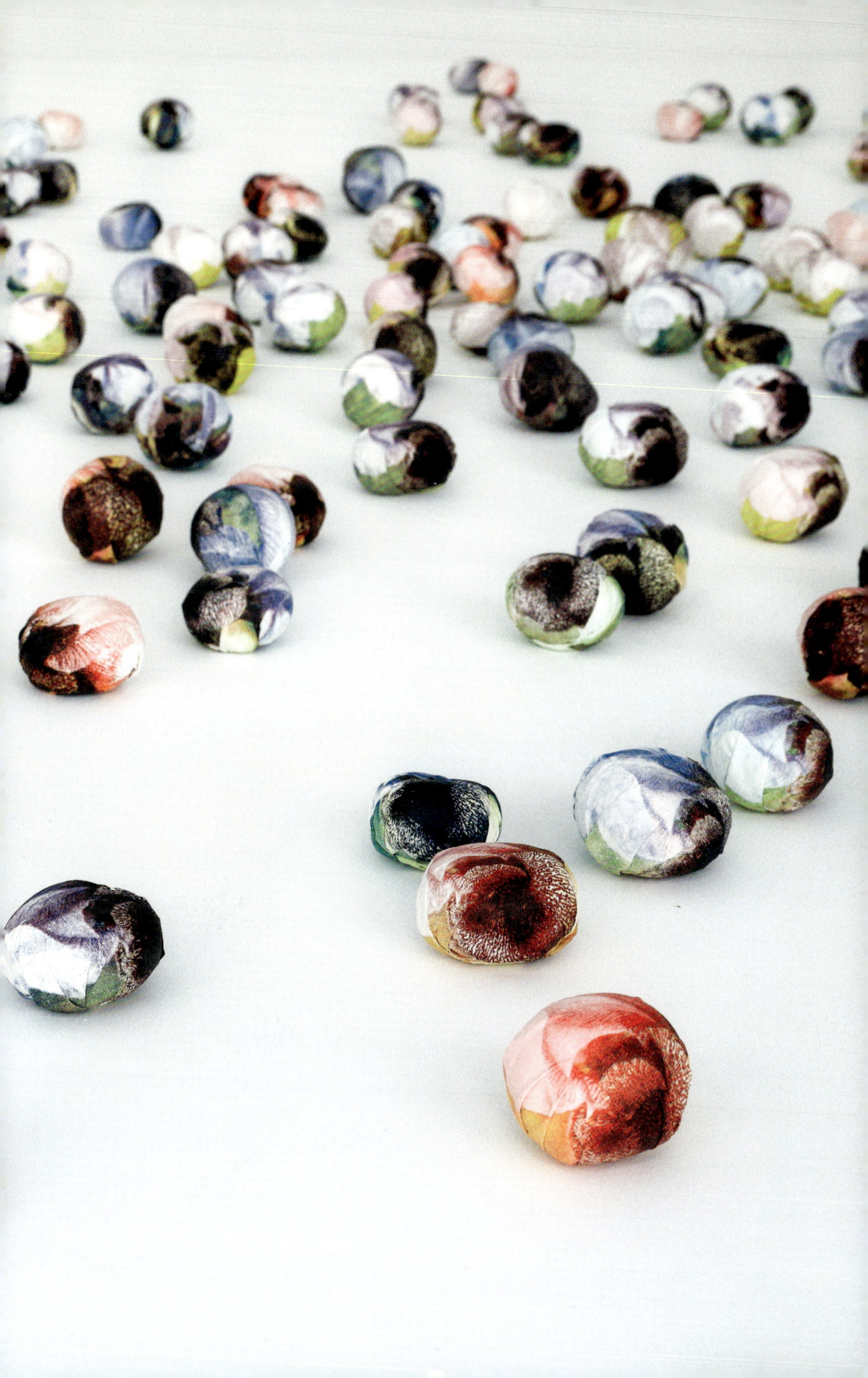

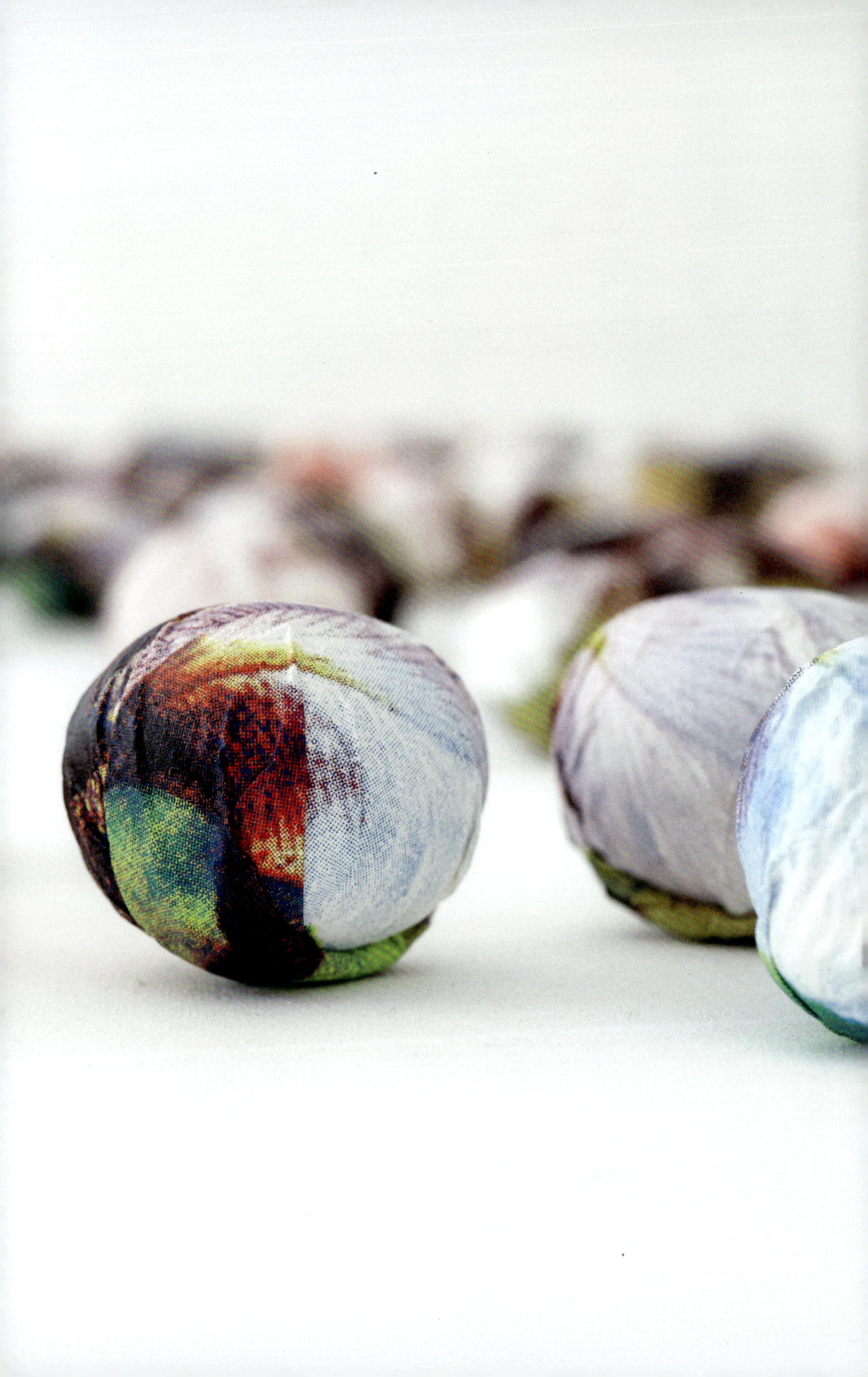

**Fatma Bucak**
*While the Dust Quickly Falls*

This book is published on the occasion of the exhibition *While the Dust Quickly Falls* at Kunsthaus Dresden 11 June – 2 October, 2022

Exhibition curated by **Kari Conte** in collaboration with **Kerstin Flasche** and **Christiane Mennicke-Schwarz**

Catalog Editor
**Kari Conte**

Edited for:
Kunsthaus Dresden
Städtische Galerie für Gegenwartskunst
Rähnitzgasse 8
01097 Dresden, Germany
kunsthausdresden.de

Texts
**Ecem Arslanay**
**Eray Çaylı**
**Kari Conte**
**Heather Davis**

Foreword
**Christiane Mennicke-Schwarz**

Design
**Esen Karol**

Proofreader
**Catherine Phillips**

Exhibition photographs
**F.B.**
[1–4, 13–16, 33–39, 43–45, 63, 65, 82–83, 86, 96, 97, 100–102, 104–105, 114, cover]
**Anja Schneider**
[26–27, 46–47, 94, 95, 99, 103, 106–111, 115–126]
**Jesse Banks III** [48]
**Tim Bowditch** [66–67]
**Beppe Giardino** [112–113]

Published and distributed by
Mousse Publishing
Contrappunto s.r.l.
Via Pier Candido Decembrio 28
20137, Milan–Italy

Available through:
Mousse Publishing, Milan
moussemagazine.it

DAP | Distributed Art Publishers, New York
artbook.com

Les presses du réel, Dijon
lespressesdureel.com

Antenne Books, London
antennebooks.com

First edition: 2023
Printed in Turkey by Ofset Yapımevi



ISBN 978-88-6749-547-4

€ 22 / $ 25

*While the Dust Quickly Falls* by Fatma Bucak is supported by the **Italian Council** (9th Edition, 2020), a program to promote Italian contemporary art in the world by the Directorate-General for Contemporary Creativity of the Italian Ministry of Culture.

The new works entered the permanent collection of **MAMbo - Museo d'Arte Moderna di Bologna**.
In addition, the exhibition is sponsored by the **SAHA Association** and the **Foundation of Art and Music for Dresden**.

**Kunsthaus Dresden** is an institution of the City of Dresden and part of the Museums of the City of Dresden.

## Acknowledgements

Yousef Shajari Aghdam, Güler Akyol, Archivio Tipografico Torino, the artist's family, Çelenk Bafra, Yeşim Bağatur, Lorenzo Balbi, Caroline Beach, Bettina Bein-Lobmaier, Laura Bollati, Ilaria Bombelli, Vinay Chowdhry, DWSI-Dresdner Wach- und Sicherungsinstitut GmbH, Füsun Eczacıbaşı, Gabriele Fumero, Dilek Gertel, Humam, Esen Karol, Şennur Kaya, Kader Kayan, İlkay Kıratlı, Tobias Köbsch, Sabine Kröhs, Sylvia Krüger, Rauf Kunt, Martina de Maizière, Meru, Robert Itz Edler von Mildenstein, Hesam Mokhber, Leyla Odabaşı, Pınar, Matteo Piccioni, Sasan Baheri Rad, Annabell Rink, Bahar Royaee, Mehdi Saadeti, Fisun Şaşmaz, Aysel Şahin, Zuhal Sardok, Christian Sylvester Seemann, Peter Segor, Besime Şen, Tom, Anna Schinzel, Pascal Storz, Anya Szykitka, Robert Thiele, and many others in different countries who helped make this exhibition possible.

Kunsthaus Dresden

Museen der Stadt Dresden

Museum der Landeshauptstadt Dresden.

K&M Stiftung Kunst und Musik für Dresden

SAHA Supporting Contemporary Art from Turkey

italianCouncil Bringing our Contemporary Art to the World

MiC Direzione Generale Creatività Contemporanea